ROYAL BERKSHIRE REGIMENT

1743–1914

EMERALD GREENS!

G.   R.

The 66th

𝕿𝖍𝖊 Regiment which Forced the Passage of the Douro!

The Heroes of *TALAVERA* and *ALBUERA*!!

𝕿𝖍𝖊 𝕮𝖔𝖓𝖖𝖚𝖊𝖗𝖔𝖗𝖘 𝖔𝖋

Vittoria, the Pyrenees, the Nive, Nivelle, Orthes, St. Palais and Toulouse !!!

THE MEN whose Valour contributed to hurl *Napoleon* from his Throne, and who carried him to his Tomb! require to complete the Flank Companies

Some Gallant and Spirited

Young Men

Who are anxious to distinguish themselves under the Green Colours of their Native Isle.

YOUNG Men of good Character and Conduct are certain of being Promoted as there are at present upwards of

FORTY SERJEANTS
AND
CORPORALS WANTING
To Complete the Corps.

NO TIME SHOULD BE LOST
As the Vacancies will shortly be filled up!

𝕲𝖔𝖉 𝕾𝖆𝖛𝖊 𝖙𝖍𝖊 𝕶𝖎𝖓𝖌.

Head-Quarters, Boyle 16th May, 1825.

Boyle, Printed at " The Roscommon and Leitrim Gazette" Office, by J. BROMELL.

ROYAL BERKSHIRE REGIMENT
1743–1914

MARTIN McINTYRE

TEMPUS

Frontispiece: A recruiting poster appealing for 'Gallant and Spirited young men' for the 66th (Berkshire) Regiment, *c.*1825. Produced when the regiment was stationed in Ireland (where it recruited heavily), the poster refers to the actions of the 2nd/66th in the Peninsula War during the opposed crossing of the river Douro. Known as 'The Emerald Greens' due to the colour of the regimental uniform facings, the 66th remained in Ireland until 1827 when it embarked for foreign service in Canada.

First published 2006

Tempus Publishing Limited
The Mill, Brimscombe Port,
Stroud, Gloucestershire, GL5 2QG
www.tempus-publishing.com

© Martin McIntyre, 2006

The right of Martin McIntyre to be identified as the Author
of this work has been asserted in accordance with the
Copyrights, Designs and Patents Act 1988.

British Library Cataloguing in Publication Data.
A catalogue record for this book is available from the British Library.

ISBN 0 7524 3914 6

Typesetting and origination by Tempus Publishing Limited.
Printed in Great Britain.

Contents

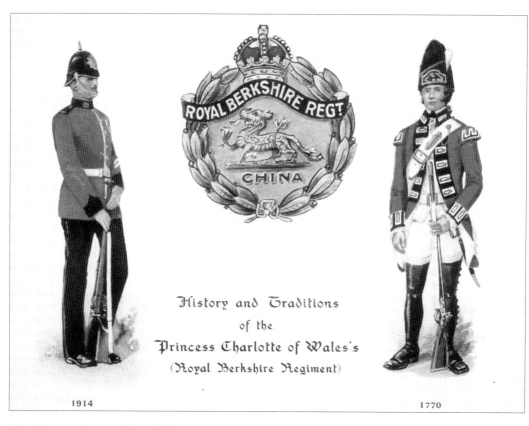

History and Traditions
of the
Princess Charlotte of Wales's
(Royal Berkshire Regiment)

1914

1770

The title page of a pamphlet published in 1914 and issued to new recruits of The Royal Berkshire Regiment, depicting the regiment's history from 1743 to 1914 through its battle honours: St Lucia, Egmont-op-Zee, Copenhagen, Douro, Talavera, Albuhera, Vittoria, Pyrenees, Nivelle, Nive, Orthes, Peninsula, Queenstown, Alma, Inkerman, Sevastopol, Kandahar 1880, Afghanistan 1879–80, Egypt 1882, Suakin 1885, Tofrek, and South Africa 1899–1902. As well as its battle honours, the regiment was also granted the privilege of displaying on its colours the device of the China Dragon, superscribed 'China' in recognition of the part played by the 49th (Hertfordshire) Regiment of Foot in the 1st China Opium War of 1840–42.

The 'China Dragon' was later adopted as the regiment's cap badge and worn until 1967, when the last unit of the regiment (the 4th/6th Territorials) was finally disbanded; the other ranks wore the badge shown on the left. The 'Royal' title, however, was added in 1885. It was later backed by its distinctive inverted red triangle, known as the Brandywine Flash.

Introduction and Acknowledgements

The Royal Berkshire Regiment began its service to the Crown in 1743. Although individuals who served in the regiment appeared in front of the camera in the early days of photography, the majority were of officer rank. Official photographic archives were not maintained and those which do survive come from sergeants' and officers' messes. Long exposure times meant that it was impossible to take the 'action photos' of combat so familiar in the modern era; most photographers had to be content with posed studies of soldiers in the field.

In the mid-1930s, the compilation of photographic albums was officially sanctioned, and a regimental museum was opened in Brock Barracks, Reading. Originally started to collect medals for the regiment and memorabilia as a training aid for recruits studying regimental history, it subsequently attracted donations of privately held photograph albums and collections. These, with official archives, have resulted in an extensive resource, containing many images that have never previously been published. In 1959 the regiment amalgamated with the Wiltshire Regiment to form the Duke of Edinburgh's Royal Regiment (Berkshire & Wiltshire). Several years later the collections from both regiments were brought together in a new regimental museum at The Wardrobe, near Salisbury Cathedral, Wiltshire. The majority of photographs in this volume are held there and are reproduced with the permission of the Museum Trustees. A further merger in 1994 produced the Royal Gloucestershire, Berkshire and Wiltshire Regiment.

This volume covers 1743–1914, with the remainder of the regiment's service up to 1959 in a separate book. Although not designed to be a comprehensive regimental history a brief synopsis of the regiment's activities is given here, in particular events that led to the wearing of insignia and to nicknames or significant regimental anniversaries.

The regular battalions of the Royal Berkshire Regiment started out as the 49th of Foot in 1743 in Jamaica and the 66th of Foot in Northumberland in 1758. In 1782 the battalions were linked to counties to assist with recruitment; the 49th became the 49th (Hertfordshire) and the 66th became the 66th (Berkshire) Regiment. In 1881, when the army was reorganised under the Cardwell reforms, the 49th and 66th were amalgamated under the title 'Princess Charlotte of Wales's (Berkshire) Regiment, becoming the 1st and 2nd Battalions respectively.

The 49th fought with distinction in the American War of Independence. No battle honours were won during this campaign; however, as a result of the daring night attack on 20/21 September 1777 at Paoli near Brandywine, the regiment later won the right to wear a piece of red fabric behind their cap badge, known as the Brandywine Flash. (This is still worn by today's regiment, the Royal Gloucestershire, Berkshire and Wiltshire Light Infantry.) Later there were many years of hard campaigning in Canada, culminating in the defence of Queenstown Heights in 1812. On returning from Canada the regiment was 'adopted' by Princess Charlotte of Wales, taking her name into its title, which remained until 1959.

The 49th was part of the British force in the Chinese Opium War 1840–42, fighting with such distinction that the honour of 'The Dragon', superscribed 'China', was awarded. The

China Dragon appeared in full or in part on the regiment's headdress badges until the amalgamation in 1959. In 1854 the 49th went to the Crimea and fought in all the major battles there, earning three Victoria Crosses in the process. In 1882 the 49th took part in the Egyptian campaign, under their new title of 1st Battalion Berkshire Regiment. This was followed by the Sudanese campaign of 1885, during which they earned the title of 'Royal' after the battle of Tofrek. Thus they became the 1st Battalion Princess Charlotte of Wales's (Royal Berkshire) Regiment. After the Sudan campaign, the 1st Battalion led a peaceful existence in Egypt, Malta, Cyprus, Ireland and England, until 1914 when the outbreak of the First World War again called them to active service, this time in France.

After formation the 66th spent many years in the West Indies. At the start of the Peninsula War a second battalion was raised. The 1st/66th served in Ceylon and on the Madras coast and took part in the Nepalese War, which later led to the long association between the British army and Ghurkha soldiers. Following the Nepalese War the battalion travelled to St Helena to guard Napoleon. The 2nd/66th played an active part in the Peninsula War, winning many battle honours. At the Battle of Albuhera they suffered severe casualties. Afterwards they joined the 1st/66th on St Helena and the two battalions merged into one.

After many years campaigning in Canada the 66th journeyed to India. In 1880 at Maiwand in Afghanistan came the regiment's darkest hour when they fought the Afghan army in the face of overwhelming odds. Over 300 men were lost and the colours were taken by the enemy. A gruelling withdrawal to Kandahar followed, where they took part in the defence until relieved by Gen. Roberts. The battalion was stationed in South Africa when the Boer War broke out. It remained and fought in that country throughout the war, gaining a VC in 1900. After the war the battalion served in Egypt and India, where it remained until the outbreak of the First World War in 1914.

The early history of the Berkshire Militia is too complex to cover here but it is particularly worthy of note that in 1908 they became the 3rd (Special Reserve) Battalion. The 4th Territorial Battalion started its existence as a volunteer battalion in 1859. Under the Haldane reforms in 1908, it became the 4th Battalion Royal Berkshire Regiment.

Thanks are due to The Royal Archives at Windsor, Catherine Hemmings, 'Roz' Robinson, Len Pettit, Roger and Rosemary Griffiths, The Royal Berkshire Regiment project group (Ian Cull, Len Webb & John Chapman), Sandra Keen, Peter Tyrell, Capt Starling (Curator RAMC Museum), Stewart Museum at the Fort, Montreal, Canada, *Military Illustrated*, Jan Ruhrmund (Morab Library, Penzance), Museum Volunteers Richard Long-Fox for the superb research he has carried out on the photographic archives. Sue Johnson for her 'eagle' eye and attention to detail and ex-curator John Peters for all the regimental advice and guidance given. And last but not least the regimental museum curator Lt-Col. (Rtd) David Chilton whose continuing support has made this project possible.

M. McIntyre
The Royal Gloucestershire, Berkshire and Wiltshire Regiment Museum (Salisbury)
The Wardrobe, 58 the Close, Salisbury, SP1 2EX
Tel 01722 419419
www.thewardrobe.org.uk

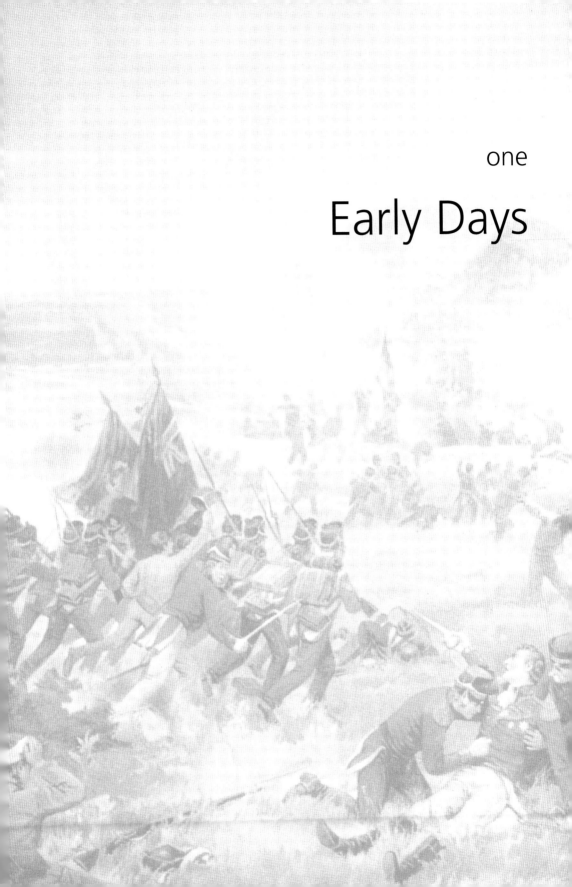

one

Early Days

The origins of the 1st Battalion can be traced back to 1714. In that year two independent companies of the 22nd Foot (later the Cheshire Regiment) were left behind as a garrison on the island of Jamaica in the West Indies. Known as 'The Jamaica Volunteers', they were joined in 1735 by six independent companies from Gibraltar and America. In 1743 these eight companies were formed into Colonel Trelawny's Regiment under the command of Edward Trelawny, the Governor of Jamaica. In 1748 they were finally shown as the 49th of Foot on the conclusion of the peace of Aix-la-Chapelle. The official birthday of the regiment is 1743. This image shows a Grenadier of the 49th in 1763.

The 2nd Battalion was originally the 66th Regiment of Foot. The 66th was formed from the 2nd/19th Regiment of Foot (later the Green Howards) at Morpeth in Northumberland in 1758, under the command of Col. Sandford. In 1782 the 66th received the county title of 'The 66th (Berkshire) Regiment'. Information on its early history is sparse, owing to the loss of the Regimental Records in 1797 during the evacuation of Port au Prince. They were linked to the 49th of Foot under the Cardwell reforms of 1881 becoming the 2nd Battalion. They remained so until 1949, when they were merged with the 1st Battalion under the post-Second World War Army reductions. This image shows a Grenadier of the 66th in 1768.

The Battle of Paoli, to the north of Brandywine Creek, 20 September 1777. A British force under the command of Gen. Grey, which included the Light Company of the 49th of Foot, surprised an American detachment, killing and capturing 400 men with a loss to themselves of only eight killed or wounded. Sgt Thomas Sullivan of the 49th later recalled, 'The most effectual precaution being taken by the general to prevent our detachment from firing, by ordering the men's pieces to be drawn that is, bullets removed from the barrels, not a man to load, and the flints to be taken out of the riflemen's pieces that could not be drawn'. With that order, Gen. Grey forever etched his name in military history with the sobriquet of 'No Flint Grey'. The Americans later referred to this action as 'The Paoli Massacre', and threatened retribution on those who took part. In response, the British soldiers dyed their green hat feathers red to indentify themselves as participants, which is commemorated today with the wearing of the red triangular Brandywine Flash behind the regimental cap badge.

A Drum Major and a Pioneer, 66th Foot, *c*.1815. The Pioneer cap bears the badge of crossed axes and saw. The regimental facings at this time were green. In the case of the Drum Major and Drummers, this was reversed, and the main body of the jacket was green. The axe carried by the Pioneer in 1815 was a genuine working tool required by all infantry regiments, both in attack and defence. Today, Pioneers in some infantry battalions carry axes on ceremonial parades. In 1815 the 66th had two operational battalions. The 1st/66th was in India, where they took part in the Nepalese War. The 2nd/66th was in England, reorganising after a very successful six years on campaign in the Peninsula War

The funeral of Napoleon Bonaparte at St Helena, 8 May 1821. The coffin was carried in turn by Grenadiers of the 20th and 66th Regiments of Foot. Maj. Charles McCarthy of the 66th later wrote, 'Saturday May 5th 1821 Napoleon Bonaparte died at six o'clock in the evening - 6th - His body laid in state at Longwood House - on the 9th he was buried under a few willow trees in Mr Talbots garden under hut gate, - 20th - I mounted guard over the body of Napoleon'. In 1816 the 2nd/66th, after Peninsula War service, joined the 1st/66th who were already on St Helena as a garrison battalion. Life was dull for soldiers on St Helena, where Napoleon had been interned after his defeat at Waterloo. Their only diversion from drill, duties and field days came when the Grenadier Company was called out to stop a fight between rival factions amongst the Chinese labourers. Soon after Napoleon's death the 66th returned to England, and after a short period there, moved to Ireland.

Pte James Smith. He was born in 1790 and served in the 66th Regiment at St Helena during the time of Napoleon's captivity. He was invalided from the Army in 1821, and subsequently lived to the age of 102 years. His grandson served in the regiment during the Boer War.

The Battle of Queenstown Heights, Canada. The American General, Van Renselaar, had assembled a force of 6,000 men, and on 13 October 1812 the invasion of Canada began. Crossing in boats at early dawn, the Americans succeeded in gaining a foothold on Queenstown Heights, which was defended by 300 men of the 49th and York Militia with a few heavy guns. Gen. Isaac Brock, himself an old 49th officer who, as its commanding officer, had brought the Regiment to Canada, was at Fort George when he heard the sound of firing and galloped off to Queenstown. He ordered reinforcements from Fort George but, without waiting for their arrival, placed himself at the head of the Light Company of the 49th and advanced to the attack. The image above is taken from a sketch by Maj. James Dennis, an officer of the 49th who took part in the battle.

Maj.-Gen. Sir Isaac Brock was born in Guernsey in 1769. He entered the 49th Regiment in 1785, afterwards commanding it in the expedition to Holland in 1799, in which he was wounded at Egmont-op-Zee. In 1801 he was present on board the *Ganges* at the Battle of Copenhagen, being the second in command of all troops with Nelson's fleet, including the 49th. In 1802 he sailed with his regiment for Canada. By 1812, when war broke out with the United States of America, he was a Major General holding the post of Provisional Lieutenant Governor and Commander of the Forces in Upper Canada. On arrival at Queenstown he addressed the men, 'Men of the 49th, I know well the trying circumstances under which you fought this morning, but the enemy have taken our gun. They will find it spiked, but it is our duty to retake it. I know I can depend on you. A foreign flag flies over a British cannon. Don't cheer men, but save your breath and follow me'. Nevertheless, they did cheer. Shortly afterwards, Gen. Brock was struck in the chest by a single musket ball, an injury which was to prove fatal.

The mortally wounded Gen. Brock urges on the men of the 49th with colours flying, together with the Canadian militia and Shawnee warriors, in the unsuccessful attempt to dislodge the invading American troops from the Heights. They were finally defeated after the British forces regrouped following the arrival of the reinforcements from Fort George. Led by Gen. Sheaffe (also of the 49th), the British attacked once more. The Americans were by this time somewhat hampered by the refusal of their militia units to cross the river, because they were only required to fight on American soil, which did not include the invasion of Canada. Taking the Americans in the flank the British regained the Heights, recaptured the guns and took some 900 prisoners, including many officers. Many of the captured 'Americans' were Irish and moves were made to transport some of them back to England to stand trial for treason. This idea was quietly shelved after the Americans made threatening noises about possible repercussions against British prisoners.

Tecumseh (pronounced *Tecumtha*), Chief of the Shawnee Indians, who fought alongside Maj.-Gen. Sir Isaac Brock during the war with America 1812–13. Of Tecumseh, Brock wrote, 'A more sagacious or a more gallant warrior does not, I believe exist'. He was admired by everyone who conversed with him. On their first meeting, after he had listened to a brief speech from the British General, Tecumseh turned to his assembled warriors and said, 'This is a MAN!', the highest and most eloquent compliment that Brock was ever paid. The Indian leader, one of the most remarkable men of his race, was commissioned a Brigadier General in the British Army during the war of 1812. When his white allies retreated before the Americans under William Henry Harrison, Tecumseh accused them of cowardice. This, and a premonition of death, made him discard foreign regalia. After persuading the British to fight Harrison on the Thames River, Ontario, the Shawnee Chief perished in battle on 5 October 1813.

The Battle of Crysler's Farm, 11 November 1813. The British force, which included the 49th, defeated an American force four times its strength. This battle was the turning point of the American War of 1812–14, and made sure that Canada remained independent. The image above shows the American forces on the verge of retreating under the relentless fire of the 49th. Eye-witnesses recorded how the steady platoon volleys, coming in deafening crashes at regular intervals, contrasted with the ragged pop-popping of the American fire. It was the 49th's last serious action of the war. The regiment was reduced to barely 100 men. Among the casualties was young Ensign Richmond, true to the grim tradition that the officer who bore the 49th Regimental Colour was always hit.

In 1959 the 1st Battalion Royal Berkshire Regiment (the old 49th) amalgamated with The Wiltshire Regiment to form the Duke of Edinburgh's Royal Regiment (Berkshire & Wiltshire). In 1961 the 1st Battalion Duke of Edinburgh's Royal Regiment were the first modern British infantry regiment to train as a complete unit in Canada on exercise 'Pond Jump'. This coincided with the opening of the Crysler Farm Battlefield Park. To commemorate the actions of its forebears, the regiment presented to the park replica colours of the 49th. Here we see Commanding Officer Lt-Col. D.E. Ballentine, MC, making the presentation to the Prime Minister of Ontario who officially opened the park on 24 June.

In 1813 Laura Secord risked her life to save soldiers of the 49th under the command of Capt. Fitzgibbon, an event which has passed into Canadian folklore. She later remembered: 'After the battle of Queenston, I returned home and found that my husband had been wounded; my house plundered and property destroyed. I learned the plans of the American Commander, and determined to put the British troops under Fitzgibbon in possession of them, and, if possible, to save the British troops from capture or perhaps, total destruction. In doing so, I found I should have great difficulty in getting through the American guards, which were out ten miles in the country. Determined to persevere, however, I left early in the morning, walked nineteen miles, over a rough and difficult part of the country, when I came to a field belonging to a Mr. Decamp, in the neighbourhood of the Beaver Dam. By this time daylight had left me. Here I found all the Indians encamped; by moonlight the scene was terrifying, Upon advancing to the Indians they all rose, and, with some yells, said "Woman," which made me tremble. I cannot express the awful feeling it gave me;

I was determined to persevere. I went up to one of the chiefs, made him understand that I had great news for Capt. Fitzgibbon, and that he must let me pass to his camp. The chief at first objected to let me pass, but finally consented, after some hesitation, to go with me and accompany me to Fitzgibbon's station, which was at the Beaver Dam, where I had an interview with him. I then told him what I had come for, and what I had heard - that the Americans intended to make an attack upon the troops under his command, and would, from their superior numbers, capture them all. Capt. Fitzgibbon formed his plans accordingly, and captured about five hundred American infantry and about fifty mounted dragoons. I returned home next day, exhausted and fatigued. I am now advanced in years, and when I look back I wonder how I could have gone through so much fatigue, with the fortitude to accomplish it'. In 1860 she was rewarded with a sum of £100 from the Prince of Wales. She died in 1868 and was buried in a churchyard in Niagara Falls. The regiment contributed to the memorial stone that covers her grave as a token of respect for her heroic action.

James Fitzgibbon was born in Ireland in 1781. At the age of fifteen he joined the 49th of Foot. By 1802, when the regiment landed at Quebec, he was a sergeant. His commander, Isaac Brock, quickly saw that Fitzgibbon was an exceptional soldier. At a time when most officers bought their commissions, Brock recommended that Fitzgibbon be granted a commission, on merit, which was duly approved in 1806, promoting him to Lieutenant in 1809. Later, Fitzgibbon received permission to form a group of men from the 49th to harass the American army in Upper Canada. They became known as the 'Green Tigers' or the 'Bloody Boys'. In 1827 he wrote, 'The weather on the 22nd day of June 1813, was very hot and Mrs Secord, whose person was slight and delicate, appeared to have been and no doubt was very much exhausted by the exertion she made in coming to me, and I have ever since held myself personally indebted to her for her conduct upon that occasion'. After the war he lived for many years in Canada. Following the death of his wife Mary, James returned to England where he was appointed a Military Knight of Windsor. He died on 10 December 1863, aged eighty-three, and was buried in St George's Chapel, Windsor. He is shown here shortly before his death.

Lt John Sewell of the 49th, pictured later in life wearing the Military General Service Medal 1793–1814 with the Crysler's Farm clasp. Born in 1794, he was the illegitimate son of the Chief Justice of Lower Canada. He was just nineteen when he fought with the 49th. He later remembered, 'The 49th had a grim tradition that the bearer of its Regimental Colour "Was always hit in action". Such had been the case at Egmont-op-Zee and also at Stoney Creek the previous June'. Crysler's Farm was a hard battle for the 49th with eleven of the eighteen officers present being either killed or wounded. Sewell survived the battle unscathed, taking over as a Company Commander. He remained in the regiment until the end of the war, reaching the rank of captain. Retiring in 1829 he returned to Quebec City, where he was appointed Gentleman Usher of the Legislative Council and later Municipal Postmaster, a position he held for thirty-six years. He remained active in the Militia, reaching the rank of colonel. When he died in 1875 he was buried with full military honours in Mount Hermon Cemetery, Quebec.

The Soldiers' monument at Stoney Creek, Canada, erected to commemorate the actions of the 49th Regiment and the 8th (King's) on 6 June 1813. The 49th was heavily involved in this battle with the British losing twenty-three men killed, 136 wounded and fifty-five missing. Capt. Fitzgibbon played a prominent part and later remembered, 'We captured Generals Chandler and Winder, one of them was in the act of presenting his pistol at a young man, Sgt Frazer of the 49th, when the Sgt raised his fuse [musket] and said "If you stir, Sir, you die". The general took his word for it and threw down his pistol and sword saying "I am your prisoner"'. Fitzgibbon went on to say, 'The Sgt stabbed seven Americans, and his brother, a young lad of the company I belonged to, stabbed four'. This commemoration took place in 1909 with the wreath sent by the Royal Berkshire Regiment Old Comrades Association on the left, and that of the 1st Battalion (the old 49th) on the right. This cairn was built in 1908 in an area known as Smiths Knoll, which was the location of the American guns during the battle.

The Brock Memorial, Queenstown, Niagara, Canada. The inscription at the base of the memorial reads, 'Upper Canada has dedicated the monument to the memory of the late Major Genereal Sir Isaac Brock CB, Provisional Governor and the Commander of the forces in the Province whose remains are deposited in the vault beneath. Opposing this invading enemy he fell in action near these heights on the 13th October 1812 in the 43rd year of his age. Revered and lamented by the people whom he governed, his loss deplored by the Sovereign to whose service his life had been devoted. A monument was originally erected on this spot by a grant from the Parliament of this Province and subsequently destroyed in the year 1838. The present monument was erected chiefly by the voluntary contributions of the Militia and Indian Warriors of this province'. This memorial is second only in height to Nelson's column. Gen. Brock is also commemorated in St Paul's Cathedral, London.

The 49th landed in England in July 1815 after thirteen years in Canada, with two hard years campaigning towards the end of that time. On arrival in England it marched to Weymouth, which at that time was a favourite resort of the Royal Family. There, the veterans of Queenstown and Crysler's Farm made haste to discard their battered campaign clothing and soon appeared in new scarlet coats, neat white breeches, and black shakos and gaiters. Everything was pipe clayed and polished. The appearance of the men on parade had such an effect on the youthful Princess Charlotte that she begged that the 49th might be 'her' regiment. This was approved, and the title 'Princess Charlotte of Wales's Regiment' was granted in 1816 and continued in use until 1959. Princess Charlotte was the only child of George IV and Queen Charlotte. In 1817, aged twenty-one, she suddenly died after giving birth to a still-born baby boy who would have been the next heir to the throne. Her death caused widespread grief and mourning throughout the country.

The 49th Regiment fought in the 1st China War (1840–42), later referred to as the 'Opium War'. On 18 May 1842 it took part in a joint attack with the 18th Regiment on Joss House Hill, Chapu, which was defended by a large number of Tartars. The commander, Col. Tomlinson, was killed; he is seen here being carried from the field of battle. Every man who attempted to enter the Joss House was killed or wounded. It was eventually entered and captured after the wall was blown in. In the image above, the 49th are advancing on the Joss House with colours flying. The regiment's casualties this day were the heaviest of the campaign with two officers and eleven other ranks killed, and six officers and forty-five men wounded. The regiment spent two years in China fighting six major battles at Canton, Amoy, Chusan, Chinhae, Chapoo, and the heights of Chin Keang Foo.

Pte John Smith, 49th of Foot, pictured here in his 89th year, wearing his campaign medals. He was born in 1820 in Killeavey, near Newry, and enlisted into the 49th in Glasgow. Shortly afterwards he sailed for Calcutta on the troopship *Minerva*. From there he went with the regiment to China, where he served throughout the 1st China War. He was still with the regiment when the Crimean War broke out. His first engagement in that campaign turned out to be his last, as he was seriously wounded as he advanced towards the Russian guns at the Alma. He remembered being nursed by Florence Nightingale at the Scutari hospital. After fourteen years of service he was invalided out of the Army and returned to his native Ireland where he became a woodranger on the Narrow-Water Estate, Warrenpoint.

A Soldier of the 66th of Foot in winter dress, by Sir James Archibald Hope. The regiment went to Canada in 1827 and remained there for thirteen years. During this time they took part in quelling the 'Papineau' rebellion and were employed on active service on the river Richelieu. In 1838 the insurgent leaders, Louert and Matthews, were captured and hanged. The 66th was then involved in skirmishes at Napiersville and Beauharnois, after which the insurgents laid down their arms. In 1840 the battalion sailed for England. This was hard campaigning, with no battle honours.

Left: Two soldiers of the 3rd Militia Battalion, *c.*1852. That year the militia underwent a major overhaul, instigated by the Duke of Wellington, with the Berkshire Militia raising 777 men. Initially, all the regiment possessed was twelve old muskets and two old drums. The first session of training took place in the Forbury, Reading, which had been used as a drill ground as far back as the days of Charles I. Joined by Regular Army instructors, the militia had regained their former state of efficiency by 1854. In 1855 they volunteered for foreign service, offering to serve in the Crimea, but they received orders to proceed to the Ionian Islands, an important garrison at that period. Remaining at Corfu for about a year, they did not see any action but lost about fifty men and nearly the same number of women and children to cholera.

Opposite below: A depiction of the 66th (Berkshire) Regiment by the renowned military artist, Harry Payne, showing a field officer and sergeant major in 1874. Although a pleasing image, it is inaccurate: the regiment was, in fact, in India and had been since 1870. It returned to England in 1881 after the campaign in Afghanistan, which included the Battle of Maiwand in 1880.

Above: One of the earliest group photographs of officers of the 49th Regiment of Foot, believed to have been taken in Ireland in 1864, prior to a posting to India. From left to right, back row: Sgt-Maj. Parr, Capts Taylor, Young and McCillan, Lt Aldworth, Ensign Williams, Capts Huicks, Cresswell and Gilespie, Lts Longsdale and Cerridge, Capt. Maden, Ensign West, Lt Mackie, -?-. Middle row: Capt. Corban, Surgeon Major Saunders, Paymaster Michelle, Maj. Goslin, Col. Adams, Maj. Armstrong, Capt. Hopkins, Ensign Arthbutnot. Front row: Lt Nason, Ensigns Temple, Fenn, Smith, Sherley, Cockburn, Carey and Bugeue. The following officers from this group served in the Crimean War: Col. Adams, Maj. Gosling, Capt. Corban, Maj. Armstrong, Capt. Hopkins and Capt. Young.

Field Officer and Sergeant Major, 66th Regiment 1874.

Sergeants of the 66th of Foot, India c.1872. Known to be in this photograph are Sgts Collins, Marshall, Williams, Cohen, Battle, Pewter, Wood, Perkins, Bartley, Abell, Haley and Jones. None of these named men were amongst the casualties in the battle of Maiwand that took place eight years later on 27 July 1880.

Officers of the 66th in India, c.1872. From left to right, back row: Addison, Perrin, Hall, Hammond, Beathie, Kelly, Avent, Aylmer, Merriwether, Saunders, Hammond. Middle row: Westopp, Murray, Sheit, Maj. Galbraith, Col. Watson (CO), Mahoney, Sandy, Pollard. Front row: Baker, Day, Browne, Oliver. Maj. Galbraith was later killed at Maiwand in 1880 whilst in command of the battalion, and Oliver died of pneumonia at Kandahar, having survived the Battle of Maiwand and the retreat to Kandahar.

two

Victoria's Wars

Above left: The 49th arrived in the Crimea in September 1854 as part of the 2nd Brigade of the 2nd Division. The Brigade Commander was an old 49th officer, Brig.-Gen. Adams. The regiment's first battle was at the river Alma, after which the British and French forces set siege to Sevastopol. The illustration depicts the action at Shell Hill where the outlying piquets of the two companies under Lt Conolly's command were confronted by a strong Russian sortie. When one of the piquets was overrun, Conolly sent a drummer to the rear to ask for instructions. A field officer gave the drummer a message telling Conolly to, 'take the responsibility [for deciding how to act] on himself'. But the drummer, who had a speech impediment, only managed to get as far as 'res-p-[responsibility]' when he was shot dead through the forehead. For Conolly, however, the message was clear; by now surrounded by at least twenty Russians he had no option but to do as ordered. Conolly fought with great courage and desperation and when his ammunition was exhausted he carried on using his sword and telescope, dispatching a number of Russians in the process. He was shot in the chest and severely wounded. For his gallantry he was awarded the Victoria Cross.

Above right: Maj. John Augustus Conolly, VC, seen here in the uniform of the Coldstream Guards. Born on 30 November 1829 in Ireland, he was commissioned into the 49th Regiment of Foot on 25 February 1848. He went to the Crimea with the 49th and fought in the battles of Alma and Sevastopol. Following the award of the Victoria Cross, he transferred to the Coldstream Guards. He was promoted by purchase to lieutenant colonel in 1863 and retired in 1870. In retirement he became a Sub-Commissioner in the Dublin Metropolitan Police, and later the Resident Magistrate for the Curragh of Kildare. He died on 23 December 1888. His medal is now in the Guards Museum in London.

Sgt James Owens, Victoria Cross, 49th of Foot. He was born in Killaine, Bailyboro, County Cavan, Ireland, in 1829. He served for twenty-one years and in retirement became a Yeoman Warder at the Tower of London, where he is shown here. His citation read, 'He greatly distinguished himself on the 30th October 1854 in personal encounter with the Russians, and nobly assisted Maj. Conolly'. He was presented with his decoration by HM Queen Victoria at her Hyde Park review on 26 June 1857. He died in Romford, Essex, on 20 August 1901.

The 'Soldiers Battle' of Inkerman, 1854. The event above was described in the *Illustrated Times*, London, in 1856, 'This battle, as everyone knows was like a huge riot, in which the attackers and the attacked, officers and men were indiscriminately mixed up together. In some parts of the field they were wedged so closely together by the advancing columns, that the only weapon they could use was the bayonet, which they dug about them like daggers. "At them with the bayonet" was the order then given, and the next moment two soldiers were up close to their enemies. One horrible crash, a sound like that of breaking bones, a shriek of pain and a Russian was on the earth, curling in agony around the steel fixed in his bosom. The man of the 49th, maddened by the danger of the day, and made as fierce as a tiger with the smell of blood, threw the bleeding Russian into the air as a farm labourer would a truss of straw on a pitchfork, and as the body came down again he caught it once more on his bayonet, in a cup and ball fashion'. It was at Inkerman that the regiment won its third Victoria Cross.

Left: Queen Victoria presents the Victoria Cross to ex-Sgt George Walters of the 49th Foot, (wearing the uniform of a constable in the Metropolitan Police) in the review at Hyde Park, 26 June 1857. He enlisted in the 49th in 1848, and by the start of the Crimean War in 1854 had been promoted to Sergeant. He fought in all the battles of the Crimea, distinguishing himself in the 'Soldiers Battle' of Inkerman. During the battle he saved the life of Brig.-Gen. Adams whilst engaged in hand-to-hand combat with the Russian Okhottsky Regiment. After the war he joined 'R' Division of the Metropolitan Police, but his time in the police was short-lived as he resigned in 1857 to take up a post at Woolwich Arsenal. He died in June 1872 aged only forty-three. He was buried in an unmarked pauper's grave in Westminster Cemetery, Finchley. In 1997, after research by local historians in Newport Pagnell, Bucks, his home town, his grave was marked with a regimental headstone.

Opposite below: This photograph is believed to be the only one in existence showing a soldier of the 49th during the Crimean War. It shows Maj.-Gen. Sir John L. Pennefathert and the staff of the 2nd Division. From left to right: Lt Wing 95th Regt, Brevet Maj. William Bellairs 49th Regt (standing),Capt. Layard, Capt. Ellison 47th Regt, Col. Wilbraham CB, Sir John Pennefather KCB, Col. the Hon. Herbert, Lt-Col. Thackwell, Staff Surgeon Wood MD. Maj. Bellairs spent most of his time with the 49th in contact with the enemy. He went on to have a long and distinguished career which culminated with his appointment as the colonel of the regiment.

Right: Pte James Sable, DCM, enlisted in the 49th of Foot in 1847 and served with them during the Crimean War. Severely wounded on 26 October 1854, he won his Distinguished Conduct Medal on the same day. This was the same action in which Lt Conolly and Cpl Owens won their Victoria Crosses. He took his discharge at Barbados in 1859. He is shown here in later life wearing his gallantry and Crimea medals, which are now in the Regimental Museum.

Pte Robert Cross, 49th of Foot, pictured here in Reading at the age of eighty-two wearing his Crimea campaign medals. He had clasps for 'Alma', 'Inkerman' and 'Sevastopol' together with the Turkish Medal and the Meritorious Service Medal. He enlisted in 1847, joining the 49th in Richmond Barracks, Dublin. His wife was the school mistress for the 49th and in that capacity served in Malta, the West Indies and at home. He was with the 49th in Ireland when the Smith O'Brien conspiracy occurred, followed by riots throughout the country. The Grenadier Company of the 49th captured Smith O'Brien in a garden in Ballingarry. In 1853 Pte Cross went to Malta, and in the following year mobilised for the Crimean War. He remembered disembarking at Scutari where the regiment was met by the band of a Turkish Regiment who 'played them in' to their barracks where food had been prepared by the Turks, but as it consisted of boiled rice and oil, the 49th did not make a very hearty meal.

Ensign A.F. Platt of the 49th of Foot, pictured here just prior to embarkation for the Crimean War. He died on 11 August 1855 from dysentery and was buried at Scutari. He is commemorated on the regiment's Crimean War memorial in St George's church, Reading.

William Livock. Born July 26. 1829 Enlisted Feb. 4. 18

Pte William Livock, drawn just prior to his departure to the Crimea. He was born on 26 July 1829 and enlisted into the 49th on 4 February 1848. He joined the regiment in Ireland but his service details beyond that are not known. He was wounded in the Battle of the Alma on 20 September 1854 and died in Scutari hospital six days later. The 49th did not suffer heavily at the Alma with one sergeant and one private killed, and one sergeant, one drummer and eight men wounded, including William Livock.

Above: The 49th returned to England from the Crimea in July 1856 with the battle honours 'Alma', 'Inkerman' and 'Sevastopol' and with three Victoria Crosses, six Legion d' honneurs, fifteen Distinguished Conduct Medals and nine French war medals. When they embarked for service in 1854, their other rank strength was 907; when they returned they were down to 654. They re-formed at Dover where they are shown above in a tented camp with the 44th (Essex) Regiment. They were fully re-formed by January 1857 when they embarked for foreign service in Barbados.

Right: The Regimental Memorial to the fallen of the 49th in the Crimean War. It was originally in All Saints church in Hertford, but after it was destroyed by fire the regiment commissioned a brass copy which was placed in St George's church in Reading, where it remains today. The monument was a massive slab of the purest Carrara marble which displayed the badge, a China dragon, colours, and military accoutrements, all mounted on a marble plinth. It listed by name the eleven officers and 395 other ranks of the regiment who failed to return.

The sergeants of the 66th in India, 1879. This is an important historical record as most of those shown would have been involved in the Afghanistan campaign the following year. Of the three dogs shown in the photograph, it is believed that 'Bobbie', the regimental pet that survived the Battle of Maiwand and was cared for by Sgt Kelly, is on the right. The following warrant officers and sergeants fell at Maiwand: Sgt Maj Cuppage; Armourer Sgt Colley; Col. Sgts Apthorpe, Bayne, Gover and Scadding; Sgts Cosgrave, Cruise, Davis, Fitzgerald, Guntripp, Rice, Rollings, Spencer (Pioneer Sgt), Symonds and Walker.

The 66th were placed under orders for service in South Afghanistan in February 1880, arriving in Kandahar in March. They remained there until mid-July, when they left as part of Brig.-Gen. Burrows' force, in an attempt to prevent Ayoub Khan's army from marching on Kandahar. Unfortunately, owing to unsound command appreciation, the situation developed, on the 27th, into the disastrous Battle of Maiwand. The colours seen at the front of the battalion were lost in this battle. Their loss, together with those lost in the Zulu campaign the previous year, led the War Office to order that colours would no longer be taken on active service. This is the last known photograph of the battalion before they proceeded on active service; it does not show the two companies who were at Khelat-i-Ghilzai.

The Fort at Khelat-i-Ghilzai which lies about ninety miles north of Kandahar. It was here, on 6 April 1880, that Capt. McKinnon of the 66th, with A and E Companies under command, took over responsibility for the fort from the 59th Foot. He was assisted by Lts Bruce, O'Donel and Fitzgerald. They remained at this fort for a little over four months, missing the Maiwand Battle. Gen. Roberts came by way of Khelat-i-Ghilzai during his famous march 'From Kabul to Kandahar' and ordered McKinnon's companies to join him, to help break the siege of Kandahar. On arrival they joined the survivors of the Maiwand Battle. Pte Preston of the 66th, who took part in that march, remembered, 'We joined Lord Roberts' forces at Khelat, many miles from Kandahar, I saw Lord Roberts practically every day. Mounted on his white charger, he came to watch his force (12,000 officers and men) pass by in order to note their condition. It was August, and the weather was very tropical. We marched from 1 a.m. through the night in mountainous country. Enteric fever and pneumonia attacked the troops, and when we arrived in Kandahar I should say that every man's feet were raw'. Pte Preston later emigrated to Canada and at the age of sixty in 1917 he joined the 140th Infantry Canadian Battalion and fought in the Ypres Salient.

An illustration of a Private soldier of the 66th (Berkshire) Regiment as he would have been equipped in the Afghanistan campaign with a white tropical helmet, fitted with a brass-link chain and a khaki cloth cover. He also has a dyed white drill frock and trousers, grey/green puttees rolled from the ankle upwards and ankle boots. He is wearing a reduced 1871 Valise Pattern with two 20-round pouches and a 30-round ball bag haversack with rations for three days and a water bottle. The soldier is armed with a Martini-Henry 0.45in-calibre, single-shot breech loading rifle with a triangular socket bayonet.

This picture is taken from Frank Feller's famous painting of the 'Stand of the Last Eleven' at the Battle of Maiwand, 27 July 1880. Sadly, there were no survivors from this last desperate encounter, but we do know of their outstanding courage from observations of an Afghan army colonel who later said, 'A party of the 66th, estimated at about 100 officers and men, made a most determined stand they were surrounded by the whole Afghan army and fought on until only eleven men were left, inflicting enormous losses upon the enemy. These eleven men charged out of the garden and died with their faces to the foe fighting to the death such was the nature of their charge and the grandeur of their bearing that, although the whole of the Ghazis were assembled round them, not one dared to approach to cut them down. Thus, standing in the open, back to back, firing steadily and truly, every shot telling, surrounded by thousands, these eleven officers and men died, and it was not until the last man had been shot down that the Ghazis dared advance upon them'. We know that ten of these soldiers were from the 66th and the remaining soldier was Lt C. Hinde of the Bombay Grenadiers.

'The Stragglers' of the 66th (Berkshire) Regiment coming into Kandahar after the action at Maiwand, as depicted by the Victorian illustrator Harry Payne. The regimental journal later recorded, 'After the battle came the terrible retreat to Kandahar. Over the wide expanse of desert were to be seen men in twos and threes, camels that had slipped their loads, sick men almost naked astride of donkeys, mules, ponies and camels. Stretcher bearers that had thrown down their dhoolies and left the wounded to their fate. The guns and carriages were crowded with wounded, suffering through pain and thirst all the tortures of the damned. With every man's hand against them the broken column plods on. Villagers from all sides creep up to the low mud walls, and many a stalwart fellow who had striven against the trials of the day and the horrors of the night fell a victim to the jezail [Afghan musket]'.

The Citadel, Kandahar, 1880, a sight familiar to the stragglers who survived the gruelling retreat from the battlefield at Maiwand. What remained of the 66th continued to garrison this location until Kandahar was relieved by Gen. Roberts on 1 September 1880 when they were reunited with the two companies from Khelat-i-Ghilzai. The survivors of the 66th played no active part in the siege of Kandahar outside guard duties. It was in the Citadel that Maj. Oliver of the 66th, who had survived the Battle of Maiwand and the retreat to Kandahar, died from pneumonia.

Surgeon Major Alexander Francis Preston, medical officer of the 66th of Foot at Maiwand. He joined the Medical Service of the Army in 1863 after graduating from Trinity College, Dublin. He joined the 66th as their medical officer and was present at the affair at Ghirisk, the Battle of Maiwand (where he was wounded) and the retreat to Kandahar. He served throughout the siege at Kandahar, being awarded a Mention in Dispatches. After the Afghanistan campaign he was promoted to Surgeon General, and was temporary General of the Army Medical Department in 1901. He was also Honorary Physician to the King. He died in 1907. 'You have been in Afghanistan, I perceive', said Sherlock Holmes to Dr Watson in the book *Study in Scarlet* produced in 1887. Sherlock Holmes later went on, 'Here is a gentleman of a medical type, but with the air of a military man. Clearly an army doctor, then. He has just come from the tropics, for his face is dark, and that is not the natural tint of his skin, for his wrists are fair. He has undergone hardship and sickness, as his haggard face says clearly. His left arm has been injured. He holds it in a stiff and unnatural manner. Where in the tropics could an English army doctor have seen such hardship and got his arm wounded? Clearly in Afghanistan'. Conan Doyle, the author and writer who produced Sherlock Holmes, based the character of Dr Watson on Surgeon Major Preston and his experiences with the 66th.

Above left: Lt-Col. James Galbraith, the commanding officer of the 66th at the Battle of Maiwand. He joined the depot of the regiment in Guernsey in 1852, and went on to serve in Canada, Gibraltar, India and Ireland. He went to India for a second time in 1870 and took command of the battalion in 1879. He was killed in action at Maiwand on 27 July 1880. Gen. Primrose later wrote, 'He was last seen on the nullah bank, kneeling on one knee, with a colour in his hand, officers and men rallying round him'. When the battlefield was revisited in September, his body, and that of his old friend Capt. McMath, were found together, with those of many of their gallant comrades.

Above right: The memorial to Lt-Col. Galbraith. His sister, who commissioned it, later wrote to Col. Ready from Drumachose Rectory, Limavady, Ireland in 1886. 'I send you a Photograph of the memorial executed by Mr Brock, and which has been erected in my brother's native parish church. The figure behind the Colonel represents Lt Honywood, that in the left corner Lt Barr. Capt. McMath getting wounded – Supports the falling body of Lt Olivey. That of Sgt Maj Cuppage is the fallen figure beneath the colour he defended to the last'. In July 1940, whilst the 6th Battalion were training in Ireland, the commanding officer drew attention to the similarity of their exercise situation to Maiwand. After a time, a signaller came and reported that he had been into a church and had discovered a marble carving commemorating the regiment. In turn, all those present went in and saw a fine bas-relief of the last eleven standing their ground at Maiwand.

Opposite above: Some of the surviving officers of the 66th, in February 1881, prior to the battalion's return to England. From left to right, back row: Lts O'Donel, Bray, Faunce, Adams, Mellis. Middle row: Lt Fitzgerald, Surgeon Major Beattie, Lt-Col. Hogge, Maj. Ready, Capt. Beresford-Peirse, Bruce. Front row: Lts Lonergan, Lynch, Edwards and Bunny. Lt Bray went on to form the 7th (Service) Battalion at the start of the First World War in 1914, in which he lost two sons, both whilst serving with the regiment. Lt Lynch went on to fight in the Sudan campaigns with the 1st Battalion in 1885, the only officer from the regiment to take part in both campaigns.

Presentation of Distinguished Conduct Medals to soldiers of the 66th of Foot at Osborne House, Isle of Wight, 17 August 1881. From left to right: Duchess of Edinburgh, Crown Prince, Queen Victoria, Princess Beatrice, Gen. Ponsonby, 'Bobbie', Sgt Bull (with Standard), Gen. du Plat. L/Cpl Martin is being presented with his medal. The four soldiers awaiting presentation are Pte Clayton, Sgt Williams (Caulfeild), Cpl Lovell and Pte Battle. Queen Victoria later wrote, 'At 11, I gave 6 good conduct medals to Sergeants and Corporals, who had, all but one, been in the 66th Regt, in the dreadful retreat after Maiwand and had shown great gallantry. I stood in front of the house, with my back to the portico, a sergeant with the colours next to me, and 200 of the 66th Regt now called Berkshire, with white facings, instead of green, under the command of Col Hogge, were formed up in a square, facing me. They had their little dog, a sort of Pomeranian, with them, which had been with them, through the campaign and is quite devoted to the men. It disappeared after Maiwand, but came back with Lord Roberts, when he entered Kandahar, and instantly recognised the remaining men of the Regiment. "Bobby" as he is called, is a great pet and had a velvet coat on, embroidered with pearls and two good conduct stripes, and other devices and orders, tied round its neck. It was wounded in the back, but had quite recovered. The men marched past, Lt Lynch was presented, who was wounded at Maiwand, and is almost the only officer of the Regiment, who came back alive'.

Left: Bobbie the dog with his handler for the day at Osborne House, Isle of Wight, 17 August 1881, after being presented to Queen Victoria. Bobbie was originally the property of Sgt Kelly. By the date of this presentation, the 66th had become the 2nd Battalion Berkshire Regiment. The soldier's tunic has the new white facings, but his 1878 pattern blue helmet, only received when the regiment returned from India, has a 66th plate from the 1869 shako, the new plate not having yet been issued. Bobbie met his end while accompanying the 66th on a route march, being run over by a cab apparently conveying a wedding party in Gosport. Bobbie can be seen to this day in the Regimental Museum in Salisbury, Wiltshire.

Below: The Distinguished Conduct Medal group after the presentation of medals for service in Afghanistan by Queen Victoria at Osborne House, August 1881. From left to right: Pte Clayton, Pte Battle, C/Sgt Woods (Northumberland Fusiliers), 'Bobbie', Cpl Lovell, Sgt Williams and L/Cpl Martin. Pte Battle joined the Army at fourteen years of age, spending a significant amount of his Army service in detention (imprisoned eighteen times) for drink-related matters, and on the day of the medal presentation was on day-release from Netley Military Hospital for undisclosed medical problems. He went on to fight with the regiment in the Sudan in 1885. On discharge his character was assessed as 'Indifferent, has been addicted to drink, but a good soldier in the field'. Cpl Lovell had previous service with the 53rd Regiment of Foot, later transferring to the Army Service Corps. His sons joined the regiment with one, Frank, being one of the first Royal Berkshiremen to lose his life in the First World War in 1914. Sgt Williams was a gentleman ranker who served under an assumed name. After the presentation of medals, at the request of Queen Victoria, he reverted to his correct name of Caulfeild, receiving a commission and transferring to the Northumberland Fusiliers, with whom he went on to win a Distinguished Service Order. He retired in 1904. He later rejoined on the outbreak of the First World War. He was killed in action at Gallipoli whilst serving with the 6th Battalion Border Regiment. At the age of fifty-seven, he was the oldest officer of that regiment to lose his life in the First World War.

Above: The Sergeant Major with members of the 66th Foot sergeants' mess, possibly taken after HM Queen Victoria's investiture at Osborne House on 17 August 1881. The only identifiable soldier in this photograph is Sgt Williams (Caulfeild) who is on the stairs wearing his Distinguished Conduct Medal.

Below: Parkhurst Barracks, Isle of Wight, 1882. Maxim Gunners of the 2nd Battalion (formerly the 66th) practise their drills. These all appear to be young soldiers, no doubt replacements for those lost at Maiwand two years before. All are wearing Glengarries, the headgear worn by all English regiments at that time.

On 28 August 1881 the 2nd Battalion joined the remainder of the 2nd Infantry Division for inspection by HRH the Duke of Cambridge, the Commander-in-Chief, on Southsea Common. It was at the time that the line regiments, to his disgust, had just lost their old numbers and were given territorial names instead. The Duke stood at the saluting base and when the colonel of the old 66th had got as far as, 'Second Battalion, Princess Charlotte of Wales's Royal Berkshire', the Duke cut him short and shouted out, '66th, quick march', after a few swear words as strong as they were audible. He rounded off his order by glaring menacingly at the colonel and calling out loudly, 'Damned old woman'.

The Maiwand Lion, Forbury Gardens, Reading, 1908. Soldiers from the regimental depot, Brock Barracks, their families and members of the public attend a commemoration service in memory of the men of the 66th who fell in Afghanistan in 1878–80. The lion was sculpted by George Blackall Simonds, one of the most outstanding members of the banking and brewing family influential in the Reading area. It is said that if a real lion stood in the manner depicted, it would fall over. To this day the Royal Berkshire Old Comrades lay a wreath at this location in memory of the men who fell.

Gibraltar, 1881. The 49th are shown here on parade, shortly after their arrival on 13 March. They appear to be still wearing green facings, which were changed to white on 6 May. On 1 July 1881, under the new rules, they also changed their title. Hitherto they had been known as the 49th (Princess Charlotte of Wales's) Hertfordshire Regiment and now they became the 1st Battalion (Princess Charlotte of Wales's) Berkshire Regiment. The three officers at the head of the colours are, from left to right: Maj. A.G. Huyshe, Col. W.W. Corban and Maj. W.J. Gillespie.

The Calpe Hunt, Gibraltar, 1883. Officers of the 1st Battalion prior to a hunt. From left to right: Lt C. Turner, Lt G.S. Swinton, Lt W.K. McClintock, Lt C. Evans-Gordon, Col. A.G. Huyshe, Lt F.B.R. Hemphill, Lt A.J.W. Dowell, Maj. C.B. Bogue and Capt. H.W. Holden. Formed in 1812, the Calpe Hunt was, in effect, run by the Army, with the hunting taking place mainly in Spain, to the amazement of the local Spanish farmers who could not understand why the foxes were not simply shot. The Hunt was disbanded in 1940. Lt G.S. Swinton was the only officer to lose his life in the Battle of Tofrek in the Sudan two years later, when he was stabbed in the back by a wounded dervish after the battle was over.

A sketch from a Berkshire Regiment officer's scrapbook showing a night attack at Suakin. The 1st Battalion arrived here in January 1885, and took up a position in the north-west of the defences called 'Sandbag Camp'. This position was anything but peaceful with the camp coming under nightly attack. The situation was made worse by bad positioning of units that resulted in casualties from jittery sentries during the night. On 12 March a major attack was made against the Ordnance Depot being guarded by three NCOs and twenty-four men of the Berkshires. Three men were killed and ten wounded, some seriously. The attackers were beaten off, with one of the Arab fatalities being Abdul Ahad, the standard bearer of Osman Digna.

Pte James Ryder, 1st Battalion. He joined the Regiment in 1881 aged nineteen, coming from Lambourn, Berkshire, after serving in the Royal Berkshire Militia for eight months. He joined the 1st Battalion in Gibraltar in 1883, going with them to Egypt the following year. He went to Suakin on 30 January 1885. On 12 March 1885 during the night attack on the encampment at Suakin, Pte Ryder was wounded. He received either a sword or spear wound to his left wrist which opened the wrist joint and left it permanently damaged. At the same time a second wound to the left side of his face knocked out two teeth and left a 3in-long scar. He remained in hospital for twenty-two days before embarking for England on the *Iberia*. On arrival he was admitted to the Netley Military Hospital, Hampshire, and stayed there until 14 July 1885 when he was discharged as 'medically unfit for further service'. He is photographed here at Netley wearing the ill-fitting and unloved hospital uniform. This was mid-blue in colour with white facings and a red tie. Unbelievably, it was still in use in the early 1960s.

The Battle of Hasheen, 20 March 1885. The image above, drawn by the war artist C.E. Fripp, shows the 1st Berkshires firing at the enemy from a high ridge. Lt-Col. Gillespie led A and B Companies up the hill, followed by Maj. Bogue with C and D. Amazingly, the battalion suffered just four wounded in the encounter, mainly because their approach was out of sight to the enemy who, with what few weapons they had,

were therefore unable to bring fire to bear on the Berkshires. Instead, the enemy fire found some of the Guards Brigade positioned in a gully behind. Two days later the Berkshires were to be engaged in the decisive Battle of Tofrek. On 3 June Maj. Bogue died of disease in Cairo.

Osman Digna's followers, who were usually referred to as dervishes, were mainly of the Hadendowa tribe. They were fanatically brave and, having few firearms, the only way they could fight was by charging to close quarters with swords and spears. In order to counteract this it was usual to build rectangular enclosures of thornbush, known locally as zaribas, which were intended to hold up charges until the concentrated rifle fire of the defenders could take effect. This photograph was taken in 1885 and these were the men who confronted the Berkshires and other units during the Sudan campaign. The warrior third from the right is in possession of a Manding sword. This weapon was responsible for many of the injuries caused to the men of the Berkshires during these hand-to-hand battles. Prior to battle many of these warriors shaved their heads. After the Battle of Tofrek, when the bodies were cleared it was discovered that there were a number of women amongst the dead.

Above and left: Tofrek – 'McNeil's Zariba' – 22 March 1885 by C.E. Fripp. Two days after Hasheen McNeil's Brigade moved towards Tamai in a two-square formation. The leading square consisted of a squadron of cavalry, the Berkshires, a battalion of Royal Marine Light Infantry and a naval gun detachment. The second, much larger, square consisted mainly of Indian native infantry and others. Slow progress forced the brigade to halt eight miles short of its destination and build a defensive zariba at Tofrek. The Berkshires were split into two different locations in the defensive area, placing them at a distinct disadvantage. Then, in the early afternoon, the cavalry screen galloped back to the zariba with warning of a fast approaching enemy. The right half of the Berkshires, still out collecting materials for their zariba, caught the full brunt of the onslaught. The resulting half-hour hand-to-hand action, so 'accurately recorded' by C.E. Fripp, subsequently received the attention of the Commander-in-Chief, Lord Wolseley, who wrote to the Berkshires, saying, 'I can assure you that nothing was talked of for days but the manner in which the Berkshires fought. All your comrades up the Nile are proud of your behaviour that day'. Royal approval came in October when it was notified that 'Her Majesty is graciously pleased, in recognition of the gallant conduct of Princess Charlotte of Wales's (Berkshire) Regiment in the action at Tofrek, to approve of the Regiment being in future designated the Princess Charlotte of Wales's Royal Berkshire Regiment'. The grant of the title 'Royal' as a reward for service in just one action in the field was then unique and probably still is. The colour of facings now changed from white to blue.

An incident at the Battle of Tofrek, 22 March 1885, between an officer of the Berkshires and a Beja tribesman armed with the double-handed Manding sword as depicted at the time by the *Illustrated London News*. During this hand-to-hand battle it became apparent very quickly that the bayonets were sub-standard and not robust enough for the task. After the battle Lt-Col. Huyshe collected many of his men's twisted bayonets for examination and sent them back to Woolwich. This resulted in improved equipment for the units that followed. Some of the senior NCOs of the battalion were less than impressed and asked for the contractors to come to the Sudan to meet the troops face-to-face. The offer was never taken up.

Wounded soldiers of the 1st Battalion at the Netley Military Hospital, 16 May 1885. All had been wounded by swords or spears in the Sudan and are shown wearing the regulation hospital uniform. From left to right: Pte Foley, Pte Powell, Pte Murgatroyd, Cpl Tugwell (seated), Pte Jefferies, Drummer A. King. Pte Jeffries was born in Harwell, Berkshire (now Oxfordshire) and joined the 1st Battalion in 1882. Prior to enlistment he was a wheelwright and carpenter. He embarked at Chatham on the SS *Australia* in September 1884, arriving in Egypt the following month. He was present with the battalion at Suakin in 1885 and was severely wounded at Tofrek. He returned to England on the *Iberia* where he was admitted to Netley Hospital. On 21 July 1885 it was stated that, 'the movement of fingers on both hands was impaired' and he was discharged as medically unfit for further service. Drummer Arthur King applied for pensioner status at the Royal Hospital Chelsea in 1931.

F Company, 1st Battalion, San Salvadore, Malta, 1888. It is believed that this photograph was taken when they were inspected by the Governor of Malta. Although it is three years after the Sudan campaign, many soldiers who took part are still serving. In this photograph thirty-nine are wearing the 1882 Egypt medal together with the Khedive's Star. At this time four companies were at Fort Ricasoli, the remainder being at Zabbar Gate, San Salvatore and Fort St Angelo. The battalion remained in Malta until 1893 when they embarked for Bermuda.

The 1st Battalion in the ever-familiar square formation, Gibraltar 1901. At this time the 2nd Battalion were learning lessons from the Boer commandos that required infantrymen to keep well spaced out making close formations redundant. Soldiers who returned to the 1st Battalion from South Africa soon passed on the lessons which continued up to 1914 when the British Expeditionary Force, although small, was sent to France as one of the best-trained armies Great Britain has ever put into the field.

three

March on the Colours

Left: The tattered remains of the King's Colour of the 2nd/66th (Berkshire) Regiment in 1936. This colour was captured at the Battle of Albuhera in 1811, during the Peninsula War, when the 2nd/66th was decimated by the Polish Lancers of the Vistula Legion, who at that time were part of Napoleon's Army. The battalion started with 400 men and in the space of seven minutes lost sixteen officers and 310 men. The following day they mustered just fifty-three men. Both colours were taken and almost destroyed in 1814 by a French mob, but were kept hidden in France until 1827. They were then placed on display in a Paris museum where they remained until 1830, when the King's Colour was taken during riots in Paris. In 1851 the Regimental Colour was destroyed in a fire during the funeral of Marshall Sebastiani. In 1861 the King's Colour was recovered from a French collector and later hung from the cornices of the chapel of the Hotel des Invalides, which is part of the annex to l'Armée Musée in Paris.

Below: Kurrachee, in the Sind District, India, 1872, on the occasion of the presentation of new colours to the 66th of Foot. Officers of the regiment are pictured here with the old colours which had been presented to the 66th without the usual ceremony of consecration at the Jesuit Barracks, Quebec, July 1851. The colours were carried in Canada, Gibraltar and India for eight years then back to England, Ireland and the Channel Islands. In 1870 they returned to India where they were replaced in 1872. At this time colours were carried everywhere by infantry regiments, including into battle, hence the tattered condition. Third from left, front row: Lt Garratt, Lt-Col. Watson, Commanding Officer, Lt Stevenson, Lt Wellman, Capt. Oliver, Capt. Cullen.

This photograph of the officers of the 66th is believed to have been taken in January 1879 at an inspection of the regiment by Brig.-Gen. Brice, commanding the Sind District. This is the only known photograph of the regiment's colours that were lost the following year in battle. Front row, far left: Lt Smallpiece, Instructor of Musketry to the Battalion. He served for twelve years, dying on 12 April 1879. Second row, second from left: Lt Garratt, killed at Maiwand. Back row left, arms folded: Capt. Cullen, killed at Maiwand. Back row, third from left: Capt. McMath, killed at Maiwand. Back row, seated, second from left: Maj. Galbraith, killed at Maiwand, as commanding officer. Back row second from right: Capt. Roberts, killed at Maiwand. Back row, far right: Capt. Oliver, survived Maiwand, but died of pneumonia in Kandahar.

The 66th on parade at Kurrachee, India, November 1879. This is believed to be the handover parade when Lt-Col. Galbraith took over command of the battalion from Lt-Col. Barclay. Nine months later most of the men in this photograph were engaged in the Battle of Maiwand on 27 July 1880. The colours directly behind Lt-Col. Barclay were lost in that battle. Ten officers and 275 men were killed, and two officers and thirty men were wounded.

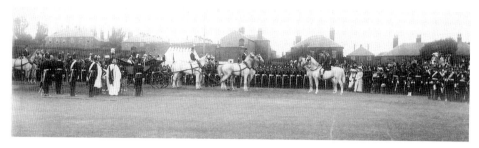

Presentation of colours to the 2nd Battalion at Parkhurst, Isle of Wight, 18 August 1881, to replace those lost at Maiwand by the 66th of Foot. HM Queen Victoria is seated in her state landau presenting the colours to Lts Bray and Bunny. In her address to the battalion she said, 'It gives me great pleasure to present you with new colours in place of those under which your comrades so gallantly fell. Your 1st Battalion is now engaged on active service in Egypt and occupies the same lines where my dear son commands his brigade. Should you also be called upon to serve against our foes, I feel convinced you will maintain the glorious name which you have earned for yourselves, and I shall always confidently rely on your courage, devotion, and loyalty'.

Officers, escorts and colours of the 49th of Foot, Gibraltar, c.1881. They remained in Gibraltar until July 1882 when they proceeded to Malta and prepared for active service in Egypt. For reasons that are not clear, the Regimental Colour was left in Malta in the safekeeping of the Governor, and the Queen's Colour taken to Egypt where it was left in the Adjutant General's office in Alexandria. The practice of taking colours into battle ceased after the losses of colours at Isandhlwana and Maiwand. The officers identified in this photograph are: second from left, standing: Maj. Fox, Lt Hemphill, Lt Alcock, Lt Gordon, Lt Burney. From left to right, middle row: (second from left) Lt McCracken, Capt. Rathbone, Maj. Huyshe, Col. Corban, Maj. Gillespie, Capt. Green, Capt. King. Front row: Lt Whittall, Lt McClintock, Lt Delamlain. By 1885 Maj. Huyse had been promoted to lieutenant colonel and commanded the battalion at the Battle of Tofrek. After the battle he was asked if he had any names to submit for awards – his answer was, 'Yes, all of them'.

Above: Floriana parade ground, Malta, 1 April 1889; the presentation of colours to the 1st Battalion by the Duke of Edinburgh, who at that time was commanding the Mediterranean fleet. This was the regiment's first presentation of 'Royal' colours following the award of the title by Queen Victoria after the Battle of Tofrek in 1885. Many who fought in that battle would have been on this parade. The colours were received by Lts Turner and Dowell. They were carried until 1908.

Right: The 1st Battalion's colours, regimental silver and captured war trophies, Malta 1889. This photograph was taken shortly after the presentation of new colours by the Duke of Edinburgh. The well-worn colours presented in 1861 are flanked by the new colours. The picture above the colours is Princess Charlotte of Wales, and the other banners below the colours are a combination of Chinese and Sudanese captured war banners. The drum between the colours is a captured Russian side drum taken during the Crimean War by the 49th. A verse that reflects the state of the old colours reads:

A moth eaten rag, on a worm eaten pole,
It does not look likely to stir a man's soul,
'Tis the deeds that were done' 'neath the moth
eaten rag,
When the pole was a staff and the rag was a flag.

The colour party with the colours of the old 49th at Brock Barracks, Reading, prior to being laid up at St Lawrence's church, Friar Street, Reading, on 7 May 1891. They had been brought home from Malta earlier by Col. Temple on his relinquishment of command. For the occasion all the available troops of the regimental depot and the 3rd (Militia) Battalion were on parade. In the church the colours were laid up over the west door under the Royal Arms. During the Second World War St Lawrence's church suffered extensive bomb damage, which also damaged the colours. They were subsequently repaired and then returned to their resting place where what is left of them can be seen to this day. Note that every member of the colour party is wearing the Egypt Medal and Khedive's Star.

The 3rd (Militia) Battalion on parade at Brock Barracks prior to escorting the old 49th colours to church for laying up. All the buildings in the photograph are still standing today, with very little change. On the right is the old officers' mess, now a Territorial Army (RRV) Headquarters. In the centre, by what was the main gate, stands the Keep, now a listed building and used by local community groups. The terraced houses beyond the barrack wall, in the Oxford Road, are still dwelling places for the local community.

The 3rd (Militia) Battalion colours and escorts, *c*.1896. From left to right: C/Sgt F. Maune, Sgt-Maj. A. Seeley, C/Sgt W. Thomas. The colours were presented on 31 July 1855 by the Countess of Abingdon, in a meadow close to the river Thames near Vastern Street in Reading. Shortly after their presentation the regiment embarked for Corfu. After the disbandment of the old Militia Battalion in 1919, Mrs Clerke Brown took safe custody of the colours until handing them back to the regiment in 1933. The Regimental Colour – on the left of the photograph – is of particular interest in that it had the county crest in the centre with the motto, *pro aris et focis* ('for our altars and hearths; for our homes').

Officers and Senior Non-Commissioned Officers of the 3rd (Militia) Battalion at Brock Barracks, 18 May 1898, after the presentation of new colours, at Windsor, by HM Queen Victoria; replacing those presented in 1855. From left to right, back row: C/Sgt Potter, C/Sgt Dodd [partly hidden], 2nd/Lt Purnell, 2nd/Lt Adams, C/Sgt Maune, C/Sgt Thomas. Middle row: Lt Royds (with colour), C/Sgt Humphries, Lt Scott, Lt Wadling, Lt Johnson, Lt and QM Brown, Capt. Nepean, Capt. Barker, Capt. Weigall, Sgt-Maj. Trinder, 2nd/Lt Packe, C/Sgt Goddard, 2nd/Lt Kent. Front row, sitting on chairs: Capt. Van de Weyer, Capt. Thorton, Maj. Gray, Col. Bowles, Capt. and Adj. Turner, Capt. Beresford, Capt. Hay. Front row, sitting on ground: Capt. Fletcher, 2nd/Lt Howard, 2nd/Lt Chamberlayne, 2nd/Lt Archer-Houblon. The colours on the left are the new colours presented by HM The Queen. The colours on the right are the old colours presented by the Countess of Abingdon in 1855. The majority of the Militia officers came from the 'County set' in Berkshire.

On the outbreak of the Boer War in South Africa in 1899, the 2nd Battalion were based in Kings William Town, the capital of old British Kaftraria. The battalion arranged for their colours to be held for safekeeping in the Town Hall together with an old drum taken from the battlefield of Maiwand. Here we see the mayor of the town, Mr J. Dyer, receiving the colours, whilst the battalion colour guard presents arms. The issue of carrying colours in battle had been decided, in consultation with commanding officers, with an Army order of 1882 which laid down that because of modern tactics and increased range of musketry, colours would be placed in a safe and secure location until the cessation of hostilities. These colours remained at the Town Hall until the end of the war.

Presentation of colours to the 1st Battalion at the general parade ground, Curragh Camp, Ireland, 14 August 1908, by Lt-Gen. the Hon. Sir N.G. Lyttelton, GCB, Commander-in-Chief in Ireland. Here we see the battalion drawn up in a hollow square where Lts A.M. Holdsworth and L.H. Birt carried the old colours for the last time while the band played *Auld Lang Syne*. The new colours were carried by the battalion until 1956 when they were laid up in Wallingford. Lt Holdsworth died after being wounded whilst in command of the 2nd Battalion on 1 July 1916, and Lt Birt was killed in action on 5 January 1915 after winning a Distinguished Service Order in 1914.

Led by Commanding Officer Brevet-Colonel W.K. McClintock (on horseback), the 1st Battalion follow their band and drums as they march past Lt-Gen. Lyttelton, after the presentation of the new colours. The Commander-in-Chief complimented Col. McClintock on the smart appearance of the men, and the perfection with which they executed the various drill movements. This was a proud day for the battalion which only a year before had been on the streets of Belfast providing aid to the civilian authorities during the riots.

The officers and their ladies of the 1st Battalion, the Curragh Camp, Dublin, 14 August 1908, after the presentation of colours. This was very much a family day with old soldiers (mainly officers) crossing the Irish sea to take part. Commanding Officer Lt-Col. McClintock, and his wife, are seated in the centre. For the soldiers who took part in the parade the remainder of the day was decreed to be a regimental holiday, with the 'wet canteen' opened for their use. The Regimental Police were fully employed during the evening!

The 4th Battalion march past their newly presented colours for the first time at Beaulieu, Hampshire, 3 August 1909. They had been designated the 4th (Territorial) Battalion the year before under the Haldane reforms and remained so until 1914 when, on the outbreak of the First World War, they expanded into two front-line battalions, the 1st/4th and the 2nd/4th. They were supported by a third battalion, the 3rd/4th at home. The colours shown here were carried until 1967 when they were laid up in St Mary's church, Reading.

The 2nd Battalion Guard of Honour for his Majesty the King, 7 December 1911, on the occasion of the Delhi Durbar, India. This photograph was taken on the Maidan at Meerut. The battalion provided the Guard of Honour immediately outside the railway station which was inspected by His Majesty on his arrival. The Guard Commander was Capt. Steele with Lts Moody Ward and Handley. Capt. Steele is nearest the camera. He was killed in action on 25 October 1914 whilst serving with the 1st Battalion. The subaltern in the centre is carrying the King's Colour.

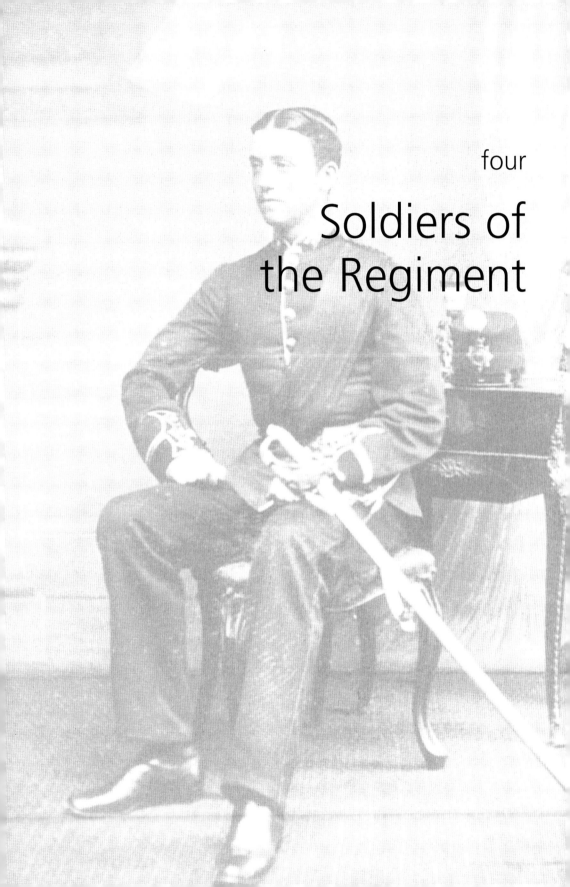

four

Soldiers of the Regiment

Capt. Conway Benning, 2nd/66th Regiment. He was originally commissioned into the Royal Artillery, but exchanged into the 66th in 1807. He was the son of Archdeacon Benning of Dromore, Ireland. Wounded twice, once at the crossing of the river Douro, and later, more seriously, at the Battle of Talavera, he recovered in time to be given command of the 2nd/66th for the Battles of Badajoz and Albuhera (the colonel having taken over the command of the Brigade). Capt. Benning was killed at Albuhera and was posthumously awarded a Gold Medal, one of six awarded to officers of the 2nd/66th for outstanding service in the Peninsula War. This medal is now on display in the Regimental Museum at Salisbury.

Capt. Sylvester Richmond, 49th of Foot. He was born in 1795 and received a commission as an Ensign in the regiment in 1811. He served in the American War 1812-14 and was wounded in the leg at Crysler's Farm in 1813, whilst carrying the Regimental Colour. Due to his wounds he suffered considerable pain and was retired on half pay. In 1836 the leg was amputated above the knee. The operation was performed without anaesthetic, and his wife sat by and held his hand the whole time. In the middle of it he sat up and drank a glass of port. At the end of the operation the surgeon examined the amputated leg and threw it across the room in disgust, saying that it need never have come off as the bullet had gone down, not up. The leg was preserved in the museum of the hospital. Capt. Richmond had ten children, later moving to Germany for health reasons, though he refused to learn German. In 1868 he was appointed Captain of Pensioners at Chelsea. He died the following year with the cause of death being recorded as 'From staying too long in his bath'.

Lt-Gen. Sir William Bellairs, KCMG, CB, Colonel of the Royal Berkshire Regiment. Joining the 49th Regiment in 1846, he became a captain in 1854. He served throughout the Crimean War, taking part in the Battles of Alma and Inkerman, the siege and fall of Sevastopol, the repulse of the Russian sortie of 26 October 1854, the attack on the quarries on 7 June 1855 and the two attacks on the Redan. On one occasion at Inkerman he led 183 men of the 49th Regiment in a bayonet charge, routing a Russian battalion who were advancing on British guns. He also served on the staff of the 2nd Division. A parliamentary return of 1857 names him as one of only 100 officers who remained present at the front from first to last during the Crimean campaign. He later served in the Kaffir War of 1877–78, commanding the combined forces on the eastern frontier of the Cape Colony. This was followed by an attachment to Lord Chelmsford's staff in the Zulu War of 1879. During the first Boer War in 1880, he commanded troops in the Transvaal and was specially mentioned for his defence of Pretoria. He was the author of *The Transvaal War, 1880-81* and *The Military Career*, a guide for young officers. He died in 1913.

Col. Sir Robert James Loyd-Lindsay, Baron Wantage of Lockinge, VC (standing). Born in 1832 and educated at Eton, he joined the Scots Fusilier Guards in 1850 and served throughout the Crimea War, where he won the Victoria Cross for gallant deeds at Alma and Inkerman. After leaving the Army he entered Parliament in 1865 and sat for twenty years as a Conservative member for Berkshire. He was closely connected with the Berkshire Volunteer Movement from its formation, as colonel of the Berkshire Volunteers. He commanded the volunteers from 1860 to 1895. At the time of the Franco–German War he founded the English Red Cross Society and personally organised and directed its work in many subsequent campaigns, including the Boer War. He is pictured here in the centre with his aide-de-camp Maj. Sir Claudius Stephen Paul Hunter, Bt (right) in Brussels in 1866, when he commanded a large contingent of British volunteers on an exchange visit to Belgium at the invitation of King Leopold. Lord Wantage died in 1901.

Left: Lt George William Monk Hall, 66th of Foot, 1865, pictured here in Devonport after returning from India. He is wearing the second pattern Albert shako headdress authorised for use in the British Army in 1855. Previously serving in the 74th Highlanders, he exchanged to the 66th in 1863. He was appointed as the Musketry Instructor in 1869 and gazetted to the rank of captain in 1873. During the Afghanistan campaign of 1879–80 he was the Brigade Transport Officer, for which he received a campaign medal and was mentioned in the Government Orders. He was compulsorily retired under the Cardwell reforms of 1881, but later returned to the 2nd Battalion as a major on half-pay, finally retiring with the rank of honorary lieutenant colonel in 1883. He died in 1906 aged sixty-seven.

Opposite below: Mr W. Brooker from Earley, Reading, formerly of the 66th of Foot, enlisted at the age of eighteen in 1876. He served in India, Egypt and Afghanistan, where he survived the Battle of Maiwand and the retreat to Kandahar. He is seen here visiting the Regimental Museum (then at Brock Barracks) where he was reunited with the Regiment's mascot 'Bobbie'. Bobbie can still be seen today in the museum's current home, The Wardrobe, Salisbury, Wiltshire. Mr Brooker died in 1951 aged ninety-three, at Swindon.

Right: Lt William Hamilton McMath was gazetted into the 66th in 1865. He joined the regiment in Devonport and went with it to Jersey and Guernsey. After twelve months at Dublin, he went with his regiment to India in 1870. Whilst there, he was attached for a short period to the 25th Native Light Infantry. On his return to the regiment he was severely wounded by a panther whilst hunting, but his constitution was such that he was able to take part in a 220-mile march that the 66th Regiment made to Poona. He commanded a company at the Battle of Maiwand on 27 July 1880, where he steadied his men with encouragement, 'That's right men; go on giving them volleys like that'. After his company was forced to retire he was struck in the shoulder by round shot and shortly after received a fatal wound to the chest. The burial party later found his little pet dog 'Nellie' dead at his side.

Drum Major Edwin Middle, 66th of Foot, 1876. He had previous service in the 47th and 72nd of Foot, transferring to the 66th in 1876 as a Private Soldier. Shortly after joining he was appointed drum major. In May 1880 he was discharged with chronic rheumatism, described as, 'A worn out Soldier', thus missing the Battle of Maiwand by two months. His replacement, L/Sgt Ireland, took over the role of acting drum major and was killed in action at Maiwand. This photograph is of particular interest as it shows the four-bar chevron worn point downwards. In 1881 it was ordered that this badge was to be worn on the lower forearm with the point of the chevrons uppermost.

Above left: Capt. T Murphy, Adjutant of the 3rd (Militia) Battalion in Reading from 1875 to 1880, retired with the rank of colonel. He lived in Reading for many years and retired to Southsea in 1895. Capt. Murphy had served in the Crimea with the 46th of Foot, exchanging to the 66th where he remained for the remainder of his service. When the regiment returned to England after the Battle of Maiwand in 1880, Capt. Murphy was selected to command the Guard of Honour at Osborne House for Queen Victoria, and accordingly went to live in a small cottage nearby, which he named 'Maiwand Cottage'. His son later remembered, 'Whilst there he had the opportunity of ascertaining Her Majesty's personal views upon that battle. With her amazing grasp of public affairs, she had come to know the inner story of that disaster, and of the magnificent show put up by the 66th. It may not be generally realised that the title of Royal, conferred on the Berkshire Regiment after Tofrek in 1885, was not given for their services in that action alone, but largely for Maiwand. Tofrek merely afforded Her Majesty a gratifying opportunity of bestowing on the Regiment a personal mark of the royal favour'. His son, C. Murphy, was born into the regiment in India and he went on to have a long and illustrious career in the regiment.

Above right: Pte Eli Thorne, 66th of Foot, a Maiwand Battle survivor wearing his campaign medals later in life. After returning to England he married Fanny Lynch in 1882. They had five sons, four of whom served in the Hampshire Regiment in the First World War. Eli died in 1916 but Fanny lived on and in 1951 was decorated with the British Empire Medal for services to Agriculture. She died in 1962.

Four young officers of the 49th of Foot, Dover, 1879. Left, standing: Lt F.W.M. McCracken, who served in Egypt in 1882 and Tofrek. During the Boer War, as a company commander he led a brilliant night-time assault on a Boer position. The hill was later named after him and carries his name to this day. In the First World War he commanded the 15th Scottish Division for two very successful years. Centre, standing: Lt E. Burney, who served in Egypt in 1882, and went on to command the 2nd Battalion during the Boer War. Right, standing: Lt W. McClintock, who served in the Sudan and at Tofrek, becoming the 1st Battalion's commanding officer in 1907. Seated: Lt A. Honeywood who, shortly after this photograph was taken, went to India where he joined the 66th of Foot. The following year he was killed in action at the Battle of Maiwand. He was shot down whilst holding a colour high above his head, shouting, 'Men, what shall we do to save this?'.

Lt Hyacinth Lynch, 66th of Foot, a survivor of the Battle of Maiwand and the retreat to Kandahar in Afghanistan, 27 July 1880. He was severely wounded at the Battle of Maiwand, having been shot whist trying to get over a wall. He was carried back to Kandahar on a gun limber. He went on to become the only officer of the regiment to have also fought with the 1st Battalion at Tofrek on 22 March 1885, during the Sudan campaign. Of Tofrek he later wrote, 'My whole company had piled arms and were in their shirt sleeves. I was cutting mimosa bushes some way out from the Zariba, and had fortunately cleared a good space. The Marines were in the Zariba in their position a little way to my left rear. When the rush came it was a toss up whether the enemy got to my arms before I did, I won and we opened fire just where we stood. I soon got my men into some sort of line and then began volleys. They drove our mules and camels at me but I downed the lot'. He retired in 1898. During the Boer War he served with the Reserve Regiment in Aldershot, and although too old for active service in the First World War, he volunteered to assist in conducting drafts of troops over to France. He died in 1947 at the age of ninety.

Lt Reginald Edward Traherne Bray, 66th of Foot, 1884, in the uniform of the Egyptian army to which he was attached at the time. He joined the regiment in 1880 and was a survivor of the Battle of Maiwand, later taking part in the defence of Kandahar in 1880, for which he was Mentioned in Dispatches. Later he served in the Nile Expedition, 1884–85, and in the Boer War. He was wounded in the night attack on the railway at Belfast in South Africa. On the outbreak of the First World War he raised and trained the 7th (Service) Battalion of the regiment. Unfortunately, due to age, he was unable to accompany them on active service. His sons did: one was killed in action in Salonika serving with the 7th Battalion in 1916, and the second, after winning the Military Cross, was killed on the Western Front in 1918 whilst serving in the 8th Battalion.

Sgt-Maj. G. Casey, 1st Battalion. In 1880 he joined the 49th of Foot at Dover, and proceeded to Gibraltar in March 1881. He took part in the Egyptian campaign of 1882, and later in 1885–86, and was slightly wounded at the Battle of Tofrek. He went on to serve in Cyprus, Malta, Bermuda, Halifax (Canada), Barbados, Portsmouth, Parkhurst, Isle of Wight, Gibraltar and Woking. In all he spent seventeen years and eight months abroad. In 1892 he was promoted to the rank of regimental quartermaster sergeant, which he held for the following twelve years until he retired in 1904. On being discharged he was appointed manager of the 1st Battalion canteen and in that capacity served in Dublin, Curragh Camp, Dover and Aldershot. On the outbreak of the First World War he was appointed to a commission as lieutenant and quartermaster and posted to the 7th (Service) Battalion which was being formed by Col. Bray. He remained with the 7th Battalion throughout the war, serving mainly in Salonika. He was mentioned in dispatches and later awarded the Meritorious Service Medal. He transferred to the Machine Gun Corps in 1918 where he was the quartermaster of the technical stores until he was demobilised in 1920. He died at Grimsby in 1934, aged seventy-four.

Lt-Col. Charles Pilcher Temple, DSO. He was born in 1843 and entered the 49th Regiment in 1862. In 1885 he was serving as the Adjutant of the 3rd (Militia) Battalion in Reading whilst his old Battalion (by now operating under the title 1st Battalion Berkshire Regiment) was on operations in the Sudan. To his delight, he was posted to the 1st Battalion and arrived with them the day before the Battle of Ginnis. Fortune smiled on him because on the day of his arrival the commanding officer, Lt-Col. Huyshe, was given command of a brigade. As a result, Lt-Col. Temple took command of the battalion and subsequently led it into action the following day. For his actions at Ginnis, he was awarded the Distinguished Service Order, becoming one of the first regimental officers to receive this award. He remained in command of the battalion in Cyprus and Malta, enhancing its already high state of efficiency. He retired in 1902 and died at Reading in 1922. Capt. E. Rhodes later referred to his command of the battalion as 'the reign of terror'. A fellow officer later said of him, 'His juniors had just a little fear of him, which was quite right'.

Lt Elmhirst Rhodes, DSO, 49th of Foot, was the brother of Cecil Rhodes, the founder of Rhodesia. Lt Rhodes was gazetted to the regiment in 1878 and took part in the Egyptian War of 1882, being present at the surrender of Kafr Dower. He again saw active service in 1885 at Suakin, Hasheen and Tofrek. As part of the signalling department of the Frontier Force, he served at Kosheh and Ginnis where he was awarded the DSO. This, one of the first Distinguished Service Orders awarded to the regiment, was presented to him by Queen Victoria. During the South African War of 1899 he was the Director of Signalling to the South African Field Force. He was present at the advance on Kimberley, including actions at Belmont, Enslin, Modder River, Magersfontien, Poplar Grove, Dreifontein and Zilikat's Nek where he was slightly wounded. He was mentioned in dispatches and retired in 1903. He was a regimental polo player, maintaining a stud of thirteen horses. After retirement he sponsored a boys' club in the east end of London and died in Brighton in 1931, aged seventy-three.

Capt. Charles Edward Howard Vincent, in 1875, the year of his retirement from the Royal Berkshire Militia. He was formerly an officer of the 23rd of Foot. He came from Donnington near Newbury and, after leaving the regiment, went on to command the Central London Rifle Rangers. He was appointed Chief of the Criminal Investigation Department at Scotland Yard, and later became the Member of Parliament for Sheffield. He was a Barrister-at-Law and a member of the French bar and was knighted in 1893.

Lt Henry Somerset Hassard joined the 66th Regiment in 1873 and is pictured here in 1879 at Reading. He remained in the regiment for many years and by 1886 had risen to the rank of major. He was appointed second in command of the 2nd Battalion in 1893. In 1898 he took a contingent of the 2nd Battalion from Plymouth to Newlyn in Cornwall to assist the local police in suppressing the Newlyn Fish Riots. After shots were fired into the sea, and one unfortunate local had his ear removed by a sword, order was restored. He died aged seventy in 1922.

Pte Charles Nutley, 2nd Battalion, who served from 1887 to 1899, had previous service in the 3rd (Militia) Battalion. He attended a mounted infantry course at Aldershot in 1891. His brother Frederick was also in the regiment, serving at Bermuda, Canada, Gibraltar and in the Boer War. Charles was a Bracknell man and he married Evline Cripps there in 1894. They had a son who was killed in the Second World War. Pte Nutley is wearing the 1878 home service helmet with the regimental helmet plate which displays a stag under an oak on the universal scroll 'Royal Berkshire Regiment'. (The background to the helmet plate centre was changed to scarlet in 1891.) He is pictured in marching order with Slade-Wallace equipment. This equipment was introduced in 1888; the ammunition pouches to the front initially carried seventy rounds, but with the introduction of the magazine rifle this was increased to ninety rounds, then to 100. On the outer edges of each pouch were two loops, so that four rounds were ready for immediate use.

RQMS E. Twitchen, 2nd Battalion, together with his wife and two servants in Meerut, India, in 1910. He joined the 1st Battalion in Malta in 1889 and went on to serve in Bermuda, Halifax, the West Indies and Gibraltar. He joined the 2nd Battalion during the Boer War and served in No.2 Company, Mounted Infantry. After the close of the campaign he was promoted Colour Sgt in G Company. He retired the year this photograph was taken. He is wearing his South African War campaign medal ribbons together with his long service ribbon.

Bandmaster A.V. Barwood of the 1st Battalion. He enlisted in the Black Watch in 1882, going to Egypt with the 'cease fire' draft. He was invalided to Cairo and later to Malta where he first came into contact with the 49th of Foot. In 1891 he went to Kneller Hall, the Army School of Music where he passed out second. He was appointed bandmaster to the 1st Battalion and remained with them for nineteen years. Shortly after joining he was appointed assistant professor of flute and piccolo. He served in Halifax, Nova Scotia, and Barbados, where he was presented with a gold watch and address by the Hastings Rock committee. In 1903 the band won second prize at the all-Army, Militia and Volunteer band contest held in Manchester, at which forty-three bands competed. The prize of £75 is still owed! In 1905 he matriculated at Oxford University, and was enrolled as a member of Queen's College. He retired to Liverpool in 1910. In 1914, on the outbreak of the First World War, when he was well over fifty years of age, he joined the Lancashire Fusiliers. In 1915 as a captain he visited the 1st Battalion of his old regiment in France; at that time he was commanding a rifle company in the line. His son also served in the Royal Berkshire Regimental band.

Sgt Ashley, 2nd Battalion, served for a full term of twenty-two years in the regiment. After his promotion to sergeant he became the officers' mess manager, a post he held for many years. He is seen here wearing his Army Temperance Society Medals awarded for abstinence from drink. The medals are The Crookshank Badge, The Silver Medal, The Victoria Medal, The Beaty Star and the Lockhart Silver Bar, indicating five years' abstinence. He retired in 1922. The RATA was founded at Agra in 1862 as the 'Soldier's Total Abstinence Association'. Its designation was changed in 1888 to the Army Temperance Association, with the prefix 'Royal' being added in 1902. Different medals were earned for periods of abstinence up to twenty years, the Bancroft Medal being the final award. Those who fell by the wayside, and many did, were stripped of their medals. The RATA flourished in the 2nd Battalion, but was not popular in the 1st.

Right: Sgt John Moody, 1st Battalion, Halifax, Nova Scotia, 1896. He enlisted in 1889 after service in the Middlesex (Militia) Regiment. He was a milkman by trade, from Rotherhithe. He served in Malta, Bermuda, Halifax, West Indies, Gibraltar and at home. After twelve years' service he was discharged as unfit for further service from the Netley Military Hospital in 1901. He was described on discharge as 'Conduct - Very Good - Invalid, very intelligent, would make a Clerk. A reliable Man'.

Below: Many soldiers took their discharge in the colonies. This group of ex-Royal Berkshire Regiment soldiers in Canada in 1911 shows fourteen of the thirty-one known to be in that country at the time. Back row, from left to right: Cpl A. Webb (Qr Mr Sgt Instr, Canadian School of Signalling), C/Sgt Dymond (Sgt-Maj., Canadian School of Musketry), Pte H. Pepell (L/Cpl 66th Regt Band and Civilian), Pte C. Mursell (Pte Royal Canadian Regt), Pte G. Hawes (Bandsman Royal Canadian Regt), Pte W. Hopkins (Sgt Royal Canadian Regt), L/Sgt H. Forwood (civilian). Front row: L/Sgt Ash (civilian), L/Sgt H. Forwood (civilian), Sgt Drummer Ivimey (civilian), Pte W. Keyes (civilian), L/Sgt W. Palmer (civilian), Pte S. Brewer (civilian), -?-. Seated, front: Pte R. Hunt (Sgt Royal Canadian Regt). Three years later, many of these men again rallied to the colours and served in various capacities in the expanded Canadian army.

Sgt Ernest Stanley Doubleday, 1st Battalion, 1905, the middleweight wrestling champion of Ireland. He joined the battalion in 1899, remaining with them for twelve years followed by seven years in the Royal West African Frontier Force (Nigeria Regiment) before rejoining the regiment in 1918. He was seconded to the Army Physical Training Corps and was one of the founding fathers of the Royal Berkshire Regiment's Old Comrades Association which he helped to form in 1908. After the war he re-enlisted as a territorial in the Gloucestershire Regiment, serving up to the age limit of fifty. On the outbreak of the Second World War he re-enlisted for a second time, this time with the Sussex Regiment, but his service was brought to a close when he was injured by a splinter from a German bomb in 1940. He was a prominent sportsman and was part of the battalion tug-of-war team that became army champions on 4 May 1903. He was a regimental historian and a regular contributor to the regimental magazine *China Dragon*. On 15 November 1949 he was discovered dead next to his bicycle in a country lane having suffered a heart attack.

Sgt Harold Thomas Forster, 1st Battalion, 1903, wearing crossed rifles on his right forearm indicating his qualification as a marksman and crossed flags on his upper sleeve denoting his battalion trade as a signaller. He was a battalion sportsman of note and played cricket for the county of Hampshire in 1911. On the outbreak of the First World War he went to France with the 1st Battalion. He was later commissioned into the 2nd Battalion, remaining with them on the Western Front and becoming the Adjutant and Battalion Sniping Officer. An officer of the battalion later described him as the best sniping officer in the 8th Division, and tells how Foster would mournfully report the death of one of his victims. 'Such a nice-looking feller', he would say, 'it quite hurt me to shoot him'. He was awarded the Distinguished Service Order and Bar, Military Cross and Bar, and Mentioned in Dispatches five times. In 1918 he was posted to the Northamptonshire Regiment as an acting Major. He was killed in action on 18 September 1918 and was buried at the Terlincthun British Military Cemetery.

Lt-Col. William Kerr McClintock, the commanding officer of the 1st Battalion, 1907. He joined the 49th of Foot in 1879, going with the battalion to Gibraltar in 1881. The next year he was in Egypt where he took part in the surrender of Kafr Dowar. In 1885 he went to Suakin, and was present at the actions of Hasheen and Ginnis. At Tofrek, he commanded A Company. He was seconded to the Queensland forces in 1891, assisting the Australian staff until 1895. In the Boer War he served in the 2nd Battalion, forming its Mounted Infantry Company. He was invalided home from South Africa, then after recovery joined the 1st Battalion in Gibraltar. Taking command of this battalion in 1904 he led them for four years, during which time he took them to the Curragh, Dublin, and the Belfast Riots of 1907. He was promoted to Brigadier General and given command of the South Midland Infantry Brigade which went to France in 1915. He was awarded a CB and retired at the end of the First World War. He died in 1940.

Sgt H. Stratford enlisted into the Royal Berkshire Regiment in 1891 and carried out his recruit training in Reading, after which he joined the 2nd Battalion, serving at Cork and Portland. In 1893 he was posted to the 1st Battalion where he remained until 1910. He served in Bermuda, Halifax, Nova Scotia, Barbados, Portsmouth, Parkhurst, Gibraltar, Woking, Dublin and Curragh Camp. On leaving the regiment he took up employment as a clerk in the Infantry Record Office at Warwick, where he worked for the next seventeen years. In 1927 he became superintending clerk in the Infantry Record Office, Exeter, where he remained until 1938, thus completing forty-seven years' service. It was in this capacity that he compiled numerous records relating to the regiment, in particular what happened to all those serving in 1914. This was a mammoth task, the results of which are still used today by researchers. He was a regular contributor to the regimental magazine *China Dragon*. He died in 1957.

Right and below: Pte William House, Victoria Cross. He was born in 1879 in Thatcham, Berkshire, and joined the regiment in 1896. After his recruit training at Reading he was posted to the 2nd Battalion in South Africa. Taking part in the Boer War, he won his VC during an attack at Silkaatsnek as a member of A Company under the command of Capt. Sir T.E. Pasley. On 2 August 1900 it was decided to make an attack on the Boer position at Mosilikatse Nek, in order to get a better idea of the enemy's force. A sergeant was sent forward to reconnoitre, but before he could rejoin his comrades he was seen by the enemy, who opened fire, wounding him most severely. He lay on the ground in full view of the Boer marksmen, who kept up a hail of bullets on and around him. Pte House, though cautioned that almost certain death lay before him, sprang out from the cover behind which he and the rest of the troops were concealed, and attempted to carry in his wounded comrade. While making this heroic attempt he himself was badly shot, and though lying fully exposed in his turn to the Boer rifle fire, called to his comrades not to come to his assistance until the advance was made. For

this act he was awarded the Victoria Cross. He remained in the Army until 1904 when he went to the reserve. This did not find favour with him and he rejoined, serving in Egypt and India. In 1911, then a lance corporal, he returned to England. On 28 February 1912 L/Cpl House, aged thirty-two, committed suicide in Shaft Barracks, Dover. At the subsequent inquest Pte Townley, Royal Berkshire Regiment, said, 'Yesterday morning, about 7.15, I was doing up my boots in the barrack room at the Grand Shaft Barracks. I was speaking to a Lance Corporal, when I heard a report from the other end of the room, I looked up and saw Lance Corporal House fall backwards, I ran down to him and saw he had blown half his head off. I did not see anything else; I called out to Lance Sgt Stroud that Lance Corporal House had blown his head off. There were six men in the room they were looking out of the window watching the Battalion march away. I ran into the next room and told another Sergeant'. The verdict was suicide. His funeral took place at St James' Cemetery, Dover, with full Military Honours, in the presence of a large gathering of friends and sympathisers. The chief mourners were his mother, his brother Thomas and sisters Daisy and Polly House. The coffin, covered by the usual insignia, was conveyed to the cemetery on a gun carriage. The deceased's company formed the escort and firing party under Lt-Col. A.J.W. Dowell. Capt. L.H. Birt and Sgt Day were in command of the firing party as the coffin was lowered and three

FUNERAL OF L.CP. HOUSE.V.C ROYAL BERKSHIRE.RGT

volleys were fired over the grave, the 'Last Post' sounded, and to a lively march his comrades stepped off to their duties. His grave remained unmarked until 1994 when the regiment, by now the Royal Gloucestershire, Berkshire & Wiltshire Regiment, arranged for a regimental headstone to be erected.

Maj. Alexander Scott Turner joined the 4th Dragoons in 1891, transferring to the Royal Berkshire Regiment in 1894. He served in Bermuda, Canada, the West Indies and at the regimental depot in Reading. In 1899 he was attached to the Niger Coast Protectorate Force where he took part in fighting in Benin and Ulia. After this attachment he joined the 2nd Battalion in South Africa and fought in the Boer War, taking part in the engagements at Zillikat's Nek and Wildfontein. After the Boer War he returned to the 1st Battalion and served at home and in Ireland. Whilst in Ireland he took part in the Belfast riots of 1907. He was promoted to major in 1911. During this time he was the editor of the regimental magazine *China Dragon* which started in 1907. On the outbreak of the First World War he went with the 1st Battalion to France and took part in the retreat from Mons. On that retreat at the village of Maroilles, the 1st Battalion were ordered to return to a bridge just outside the village and either take it or hold the German advance. Maj. Turner was in command of B Company. As they advanced on the bridge he was approached by some troops who appeared to be French, and asked him,

in English, if he had a map. He obliged, but the troops turned out to be German, and one of them drew a revolver, wounding the major and taking him prisoner. For Maj. Turner the war was over, and he spent the next four years as a Prisoner of War in various camps in Germany. At the end of the war he returned to Reading and thereafter assisted in re-forming the 1st Battalion at Chisledon. He retired in September 1919.

In 1899, then a Lieutenant, Alexander Scott Turner was the officer in command of a detachment of the Niger Protectorate Force when they captured a local chief. The chief, called Ologboshire, had been responsible for the Benin Massacre in January 1897, when seven European officials and a number of local natives were killed. Following the occupation of Benin City by the punitive expedition in 1897, Ologboshire escaped into the bush with two of his subordinate chiefs, Abohan and Oviaware, where he organised an uprising. This uprising was put down by the Benin territories expedition in 1899. Here, two native soldiers from Lt Turner's command guard the prisoner. Shortly after this photograph was taken, Ologboshire was tried and hanged. Oviaware was killed in action. Abohan was captured alive, but was not convicted of complicity in the massacre. These short, but sharp, expeditions and actions were very useful for young officers to practise their command skills under active service conditions.

Capt. George William Patrick Dawes, 2nd Battalion. He was commissioned into the regiment in 1901, serving in the Boer War. After developing a very strong interest in flying he attended a ballooning course in Aldershot whilst on leave from India. He took up flying in 1909 and was issued with a pilot's licence, number 17, being the first officer in the British army to be awarded an aviator's certificate. Transferring to the Royal Flying Corps on its formation in 1912, he was in the first contingent of RFC officers to move to France in 1914. He was active during the retreat from Mons as a flight commander in No.2 Squadron. On 22 August 1914 he was flying as an observer in a BE2a, when the first German aircraft seen in the war, an Albatross biplane, was encountered over the RFC aerodrome at Maubeuge. From 1916 to 1918 he commanded the RFC detachment in the Balkans. He was awarded the DSO in 1917 and was Mentioned in Dispatches seven times. During the Second World War he served as a wing commander. He died in 1960.

The recalled reservist. Most soldiers who joined after the Boer War and before the commencement of the First World War served seven years with the colours followed by five years on the reserve. The seven years were spent either at home or in far-flung outposts of the British Empire, engaged in peacetime soldiering. After demob most would claim to have 'done their bit'. One such soldier was Pte John Thomas Pizzey who was born in Sudbury in 1890, joining the Royal Berkshire Regiment in 1904. By 1911 he completed his service with the colours and returned to civilian life, taking up his occupation as a labourer and getting married. On the outbreak of war he was recalled to the colours and went to France on 31 August 1914, joining the 1st Battalion where he took part in the retreat from Mons and qualified for the 1914 Star, sometimes referred to as Mons Star. In 1916 he was wounded and is pictured here in the centre making his way to the rear with a fellow wounded soldier and a German prisoner of war.

five

Barrack
Life

The Volunteer Force came into being in 1859 in response to fears of a French invasion. At first the units, raised under the provisions of an act of 1804, were independent, with little coordination between them. In 1863 the Volunteer Act was passed and the battalion became the First Administrative Battalion Berkshire Rifle Volunteers. Here we see the Berkshire Rifle Volunteers at Crookham, near Marlow, in 1863, having a kit inspection. Col. Sir Robert Lloyd Lindsay VC is standing with his arms behind his back. He had raised the Berkshire Volunteers three years earlier, with himself in command. By 1861 the various sub-units became organised into the newly constituted Berkshire Volunteer Administrative Battalion with companies located at Reading (three), Windsor (two) and one each at Newbury, Abingdon, Maidenhead and Wantage, with sub-divisions at Wokingham, Windsor Forest, Faringdon, Winkfield, Wallingford, and Sandhurst.

The Berkshire Volunteers at camp at Crookham, near Marlow, in 1863. The officer seated in the centre is Col. Sir Robert Lloyd Lindsay VC (later Lord Wantage); he had won his Victoria Cross in the Crimea War as an officer in the Scots Fusilier Guards. Standing behind him (next to the Cup) is believed to be Lt Morland of the brewing family. Many of the officers of the volunteers contributed financially towards the upkeep of their own battalions.

The barracks of the 66th Foot at Karachi, India (now Pakistan) in 1879. The regiment arrived in these barracks in December 1878, relieving the 83rd (County of Dublin) Regiment who had been ordered on active service. It was from these barracks that the regiment embarked on operations to Afghanistan, including the Battle of Maiwand in 1880. Like all barrack blocks in the tropics at that time they were large, well-built buildings with very high ceilings to allow the air to circulate.

Until the 1870s Infantry Regiments had no permanent depots; each battalion had one or more depot companies which it left behind in the United Kingdom when it went on foreign service. It was not until 25 January 1878 that the depot companies of the 49th and 66th Regiments moved into the splendid new barracks in Reading, being linked three years later to form the 1st and 2nd Battalions under the Cardwell reforms. Here we see a recruit squad at Brock Barracks, Reading, in the late 1890s. Training was hard: as soon as it was light they drilled from 6.30 to 7.30 a.m., and also 9 to 10, 11 to 12, and 2 to 3 p.m. At 3.30 p.m. they went to school for an hour, then at 5.30 p.m., for half an hour, it was gymnastics. The sergeant instructor (right) is wearing the medals of the Egyptian campaigns with the Khedive's Star. Directly behind him is a building recognisable today as 'The Dragon Club' used by the Royal Berkshire Old Comrades Association.

1st Battalion polo team, Malta, c.1886. From left to right: Capt. Edwards, Lt Turner, Lt Feetham, Capt. Hemphill. This team competed against six other battalions on the island, plus the Royal Navy. The battalion won the Polo Cup each year that they competed. They were well off for ponies: Capt. Turner had seventeen and the regiment had forty-six. Capt. Hemphill was later killed in a polo accident in Malta in 1891. Lt Feetham was killed in France in March 1918, when he was a Major General commanding the 46th Division. After Capt. Turner retired he became a great supporter of cricket in Berkshire and was Honorary Secretary of the County Club. He died in 1926.

Officers' batmen, [servants] 1st Battalion, Pembroke Camp, Malta, c.1886. Each was responsible for ensuring his officer was well turned out. In return, most officers made sure that their own batman was well looked after. These men also doubled as officers' mess waiters at the larger Mess functions. All these men are older soldiers and no doubt would have taken part in the recent Sudan campaign.

Above: Ambulance Company, 1st Volunteer Battalion, 1889. Most of the men shown would have been local to Reading. These soldiers are wearing glengarries which are normally associated with Scottish regiments. This practice was discontinued by English regiments in the early 1890s. The badge on the right arm of the soldier standing on the left identifies him as a bugler. Later the duties of stretcher bearers and battlefield medical orderlies were taken on by the band. The Volunteer Battalion became the 4th Battalion in 1908.

Below: The officers of the 1st Battalion, Malta, 1891. From left to right, back row: 2nd Lt Maurice, 2nd Lt Hogg, Lt Betty, Capt. Holden, Lt Swinton, Capt. Hemphill, Lt Finch, Capt. Lee, Capt. Fitzherbert, Lt Moore, Lt MacDonnell, Lt Barlow. Middle row: Lt Arbuthnot, Lt (QM) Ford, Maj. Hassard, Maj. Dickson, Col. Temple DSO, Maj Collings, Lt Cave, Maj McCracken, Lt Foley, Capt. Chase. Front row: 2nd Lt Holden, 2nd Lt Ward, Lt Taylor. Six years earlier, at the Battle of Tofrek, Lt (QM) Ford had a

narrow escape when, after being pursued by Mahdi tribesmen, who were gaining on him, he ran towards the Royal Marine Light Infantry square. However, his position was such that the Marines could not open fire for fear of hitting him. Then, just as he was about to be cut down, Lt Ford tripped over a bush and fell flat on his face, and a Marine volley crashed out over his head, chopping down the men chasing him.

Above: Officers of the 49th Regimental District at Brock Barracks, Reading, 1898. From left to right: Capt. C. Turner (Adjutant), Lt H. Newbould, Col E. Dickson (officer commanding), Capt. L. Weigall, Lt A.S. Turner, Lt and QM T. Brown, Maj. H. Lynch. Col. Dickson later became the Colonel of the Regiment in 1914 at the outbreak of the First World War. Lt Brown joined the 49th in 1879. In Egypt, in 1882, he served in the mounted infantry, fighting in the actions at El-Magfar, Tel-el-Muhuta, Mahsama, both actions at Kassassin, and Tel-el-Kebir. In 1885 he returned to the Sudan where he saw action at Suakin, Hasheen, Tofrek and Ginnis. Maj. Lynch was the only officer of the regiment to have fought at both Maiwand, (where he was badly wounded), and Tofrek.

Below: Sergeants of the 49th Regimental District pictured in Brock Barracks, *c*.1898. From left to right, back row: L/Sgt Fitchett, Sgts Thomas, Middleton, Bedding, L/Sgts Crayford, Griffin. Second row: Sgt Seaton, L/Sgt Pepin, Sgts Roberts and Cox, Bandmaster Nixon, Sgts O'Conner and Knott, C/Sgts Goddard, Merritt and Reynolds. Third row: L/Sgt Cane, C/Sgts Trinder, Humphries, Prater

and Potter, Mr Boshell (schoolmaster), C/Sgts Parmenter, Hounsell and Patterson. Front row: Sgt Balfour (Army Pay Corps), Sgt Drummer Spencer, Sgt Inst Musketry Wood, Sgt Simpson (APC), Sgt Maj Beal, Capt. and Adj. Turner, Sgt-Maj. Seely, Qr Master Sgt Davis, Col./Sgt Leavy, Qr Master Sgt McKenna (APC), Qr Master Sgt Hall. Most of those shown would have served in both the 1st and 2nd Battalions.

Above: Commanding Officer Lt-Col. Dickson, Adj. Lt Maurice, and Sgts Mess, 2nd Battalion, Happy Valley, Bermuda, March 1895. In 1894 Rudyard Kipling visited the battalion where he spent an evening in the sergeants' mess. Most of the sergeants would have been young soldiers fourteen years previously when the 66th made its heroic stand at Maiwand. As a result of speaking with these men, Kipling wrote a ballad called 'That day' which recorded the disaster:

> It got beyond all orders 'an it got beyond all 'ope;
> It got to shammin' wounded an' retirin' from the 'alt.
> 'Ole companies was looking' for the nearest road to slope;
> It were just a bloomin 'knock–out–an' our fault!
> Now there ain't no chorus 'ere to give,
> Nor there ain't no band to play;
> An ' I wish I was dead 'fore I done what I did,
> Or what I seed that day!

Below: The *Pavonia*, a hired troopship that carried the 1st Battalion from Bermuda to Halifax in 1895. The journey took three days. On arrival at Halifax the battalion was quartered in Wellington Barracks, having relieved the 8th King's Liverpool Regiment. The *Pavonia* was built for the Cunard Steam Ship Co. by J. & G. Thomson of Glasgow in 1882. With room for 200 first-class and 1,500 third-class passengers, the vessel was able to accommodate a complete battalion quite easily. After being used as troop transport for the Boer War, she was scrapped in 1900.

In 1867 the British North America Act was passed, creating the Federations that form Canada today. As a result, the British Army withdrew into the garrisons at Esqimault and Halifax. The fortifications at Halifax formed one element of the so-called British Marine Quadrilateral (Malta, Gibraltar, Bermuda and Halifax). Here we see the band of the 1st Battalion practising outside the living quarters at Wellington Barracks, Halifax, Nova Scotia, in the summer of 1896. The barracks had high ceilings and large airy spaces, said to have been the consequence of a mix-up in specifications between the West Indies and Canada.

The Citadel, Halifax. One company was quartered at Glacis Barracks, shown here, with the remainder in Wellington Barracks. The Royal Berkshire sentry can be seen still wearing his white tropical helmet. The Citadel was built in 1856 and is an excellent example of a nineteenth-century bastion fortification complete with defensive ditch, ramparts, musketry gallery, powder magazine and signal masts. Although never attacked, the fort was garrisoned by the British Army until 1906. Today the Citadel is cared for by Parks Canada and is recognised as one of the most important historic sites in that country.

Officers of the 1st Battalion, Halifax, Nova Scotia, 1896. From left to right, back row: Capt. Chase, Lt Turner, Lt Annesley, Lt Neve. Second row: Lt Finch, Lt and Quartermaster Redstone, Lt Hincks, Lt Striedinger, Capt. Fitzherbert, Capt. Wigan, Lt Barlow, Lt Foley, Lt and Adj. Maurice. Third row: Lt Kemmis-Betty, Capt. Cave, Maj. Evans-Gordon, Lt-Col. Collings, Maj. Edwards, Maj. De La Faunge. Bottom row: Lt Ellis, Lt Lees, Lt Macdonald. The officers took full advantage of any hunting and fishing the posting offered, occasionally travelling as far as the United States to do so.

On arrival at Halifax the battalion was issued with winter clothing. As well as woollen underwear and scarves, they received long leather boots fitting well up to the knee to which a pair of steel 'creepers' could be attached for better grip. Their wool-lined leather gloves had only the forefinger and thumb of the right hand separate from the remainder in order that the rifle might be grasped and fired. Bearskin hats that could be turned down round the neck and ears and tied under the chin leaving only the eyes, nose and mouth exposed to the weather completed their protection. After several years in the Caribbean the clothing was more than welcome.

A battalion snow-clearing fatigue at Wellington Barracks, Halifax, *c.*1898. The climate was a bit of a shock to the system after many years in Bermuda. The winters were severe with the temperature sometimes 34 degrees (farenheit) below zero, but the dry atmosphere tended to keep everyone healthy. During the winter period, training was carried out inside the barrack verandas which had heaters. It seems as though a snowball fight had just taken place with order being restored by the sergeant on the left who would appear to have received several direct hits himself.

1st Battalion, Halifax, Nova Scotia, 1898. The men are taking their meal break during training on McNabs Island, near Halifax. Sgt-Maj. Beesley later remembered, 'Two companies at a time went there for musketry. When firing had finished for the day men would wander about the woods, go fishing, or late in the summer gather raspberries or blue berries, growing wild in profusion. Dab fishing and winkle gathering were also great pastimes, the odour of frying fish and boiling winkles pervaded the whole camp every evening. The annual course of musketry at McNabs was altogether a pleasant holiday'. Today, Parks Canada are responsible for what is now a tourist attraction.

Above and below: Although the majority of time spent in the UK was taken up with training and routine matters, there were occasions when the regiment was called upon to take a more active role and was quartered in unexpected locations. In May 1896 riots erupted in the fishing village of Newlyn, Cornwall, caused by Yarmouth fishermen landing their catches on a Sunday. The local police were unable to contain the situation and the government of the day called on the army and navy for help. It came in the shape of the 2nd Battalion Royal Berkshire Regiment, who were at that time stationed at Plymouth, and three naval vessels, HMS *Ferret*, HMS *Traveller* and HMS *Curlew*. The Royal Berkshire contingent consisted of Maj. Hassard, ten officers and 300 men. The above photograph shows soldiers of the regiment in New Road, Newlyn, en route to Penzance. On the officer's left is Mr George Bazeley, JP, whose function was to read the 'Riot Act' if required. The photograph below shows soldiers in a more relaxed mode on the quay at Newlyn. A local newspaper reported, 'Three Lowestoft boats in the bay were making for Newlyn, but being warned by the soldiers firing in the water they kept off. About eight o'clock when the police were being hooted and the local fishermen were gathering in dangerous crowds, the military started.

Cheers marked their progress towards Newlyn, but after they had crossed the bridge leading to the village these gave way to hissing, hooting, yelling and screeching from the masses of fishermen, through which the "the thin red line" made its way. From all quarters stones came flying amongst the soldiers, and attempts were made to trip them'. Further reports stated that during the entry of the 2nd Battalion several casualties occurred. One man had his ear cut off by either an officer's sword or a bayonet; one had a bayonet thrust through his ear, while another, who attempted to interfere, was struck with the butt end of a rifle. The battalion remained for a few weeks until order was restored.

The 1st Battalion's farewell pantomime to Malta, 1893. It was organised by Lt Moore (seated centre) who wrote the extravaganza 'Aladdin and the Lamp'. He designed all the costumes, took charge of all the stage arrangements, and directed the play. Sgt Devaney was 'Widow Twanky' and the 'Princess' was a young English girl from a café in Strada Reale. Sgts Lavington and Border played two automatons singing a popular song of the day, *Put a Penny in the Slot*. The event played for three nights to packed houses. All who saw it agreed that the battalion had excelled itself in its final performance.

A rifle section of the 2nd Battalion on exercise, *c.*1897. The battalion at this time was based in Talavera Barracks, Aldershot, but spent a significant amount of time under canvas. This photograph was taken near Aylesbury in Buckinghamshire. They are all wearing the home service uniform with Slade Wallace equipment. The only identifiable soldier in this group is Pte Jim Slade (kneeling front right) who came from North Moreton in Berkshire. He enlisted on 2 June 1897, went on to serve in the Boer War and was discharged in 1903 to the Militia.

A Guard of Honour of the 1st Battalion, headed by the Corps of Drums, return to South Barracks, Gibraltar from Ragged Staff'; the Battalion Headquarter Guard sentry can be seen presenting arms. South Barracks, like all barracks in hot climates, was solidly built with high rooms to allow the free circulation of air.

The cooks of the 1st Battalion, Gibraltar, 1901. It was around this time that the British Army moved away from soldiers eating in company barracks towards a more centralised messing system, which necessitated a more professional approach in the art of producing edible food. However, it took a further forty years before the Army Catering Corps was formed.

A regimental picnic party to Algeciras, Spain, 1902. The married families were occasionally allowed to spend some leisure time in Spain and here we see a 1st Battalion party about to depart from Gibraltar. RSM Beesley later remembered, 'The commanding officer arranged an outing for all the married folk of the regiment, the band and drums, and many others went to the cork woods in Spain. Crossing to Algeciras by boat, from there the party went by special train several miles inland. It was a most enjoyable outing, refreshments of all kinds were provided, there were games and sports, with special sports for the youngsters and good music. Everybody was sorry when evening approached, the bugle sounded the retire, and the return to the Rock was made'. Quite what the ladies thought about acting on a bugle call is not recorded.

Whilst the officers and married men enjoyed the delights of Spain on excursions many of the single soldiers, which formed the majority within the battalion, spent an amount of time in what was referred to as 'the wet canteen'; this was no more than a drinking den where the battalion's hardened drinkers spent many hours until alcoholic oblivion or the Regimental Police overtook them. The temperance societies which were active in civilian life at this time were also active within the Army. It is recorded that the temperance society was not very successful within the 1st Battalion, which this picture, showing soldiers of the D Company relaxing in Gibraltar, seems to confirm.

An interesting group of warrant officers and sergeants, 1st Battalion, Gibraltar, 1901. They are wearing the newly issued 'Douro' headdress badge. Seated on the left is the pioneer sergeant, the only man allowed to sport a beard. His specialist badge, the crossed axes, are worn on his right arm above the chevrons. Sgt Lickman (seated second from right) was later commissioned, becoming the quartermaster of the 2nd Battalion.

Transport Section, 2nd Battalion, Egypt, c.1904. All infantry regiments at this period had a considerable horse presence. The county of Berkshire was almost entirely rural at that time, so skilled men to ride the horses were readily available. Most of these men were older soldiers who had spent the majority of their earlier service in rifle companies, so the appeal of the Transport Section to infantrymen was obvious.

Above: Football team, 1st Volunteer Battalion, at Reading, 1906–07. From left to right, back row: Sgt Smith, Sgt Barley, C/Sgt Reynolds, Sgt Bugler Davey. Second row: Sgt Kirby, Sgt Maj Shingler, Pte Griffin, Pte Stone, Pte Buss, Cpl Baggaley, Pte Sallery. Third row: Pte Staveley, Pte Appleby, Pte Bennett, Capt. Cooper, Pte Romain, Pte Weller, Pte Mills. Front row: Pte Dutton, Pte Beasley (team captain), Pte Whitchelo. Capt. Cooper served in the Berkshire Volunteer battalions for thirty-seven years.

Above: 'Uniforms of the Regiment'. Inkerman Barracks, Woking, Surrey, 1902–04, showing different types of dress worn in the barracks at that time. From left to right: Pioneer Pte Holloway, Drummer Thompsett, Sgt Drummer Lavington, Drummer boy –?–, Sgt-Maj. Bestley, C/Sgt Cane, Gym Sgt Cook, bandsman –?–, Quartermaster Sgt Boshell. Members of the Boshell family provided several generations of service to the Royal Berkshire Regiment. QMS Boshell was later commissioned and won the DSO in the First World War. His son was also commissioned into the regiment and he, too, won the DSO, this time in Burma during the 2nd World War.

Below: A group of senior Non-Commissioned officers together with two officers, Inkerman Barracks, Woking, 1904. The sergeants are all wearing the much-hated Brodrick cap which was discontinued shortly after. In the back row on the left is Sergeant Foster (Commissioned during the First World War where he was awarded the DSO and Bar, MC and Bar. He was mentioned in dispatches five times but was killed in action on 18 September 1918). Sitting on the right is Sgt Godden and on the left is C/Sgt Lainsbury (Distinguished Conduct Medal in the First World War with the 8th Service Battalion).

Opposite below: Sergeants, their ladies and children of the 2nd Battalion, during a sports day at Meerut, India, 27 December 1909. Only a limited number of married soldiers were allowed to have their wives accompany them on these overseas posting. The ladies were encouraged to take part in all suitable regimental activities.

The wedding group of Sgt Levy of the 1st Battalion, 1903. The wedding took place in Reading at a time when the battalion was stationed at nearby Inkerman Barracks, Woking, Surrey. It appears that his best man is Sgt Godden who is standing directly behind him.

E Company, 1st Battalion 'Cubiclemen', Inkerman Barracks, Woking, 1904. Later generations would call them 'barrack room orderlies'. From left to right, back row: Pte Allsworth, Pte Lamble, Pte Wells, L/Cpl Justice, Pte Spencer. Front row: Pte Partridge, Pte Korkett, Cpl Annetts, Pte Hill. The function of the 'Cubiclemen' was to keep the barrack room clean and secure during the day in the absence of the men on training. Pte Wells was killed in action on 14 November 1914 during the first Battle of Ypres.

The guard room for the 2nd Battalion, Meerut, India, 1912. Whilst most soldiers posted abroad sent postcards to their loved ones showing local scenery, it appears the soldiers of this battalion thought the guard room fitted the bill. Like most pre-First World War battalions, many of the soldiers frequented this establishment on a regular basis.

The Regimental Police, 2nd Battalion, Meerut, India, 1910. All are wearing long-service chevrons on their lower left sleeves. The regimental title is visible on their helmets. To a man they would have been capable of enforcing the required discipline in the regimental wet canteen.

Capt. Robert Bruce Swinton's funeral procession, Inkerman Barracks, Woking, 1904. Born in Madras, India in 1864, he was commissioned into the Royal Berkshire Regiment in 1886. He served in Egypt, Cyprus, Bermuda, Malta and at home. During the Boer War he was seconded to the 3rd Royal West Sussex Regiment and was mentioned in dispatches twice. He was qualified as a Musketry and Signals instructor. A brass memorial to his memory is located in the old Regimental Garrison church, St George's Road, Reading.

The 1st Battalion Band and Drums under Sgt Barrett playing Stienburgh's Funeral March, on route from Shaft Barracks, Dover, to St James' Cemetery on 28 February 1912 at the funeral of L/Cpl House VC. The battalion remained in Shaft Barracks until 28 September 1913 when they transferred to Mandora Barracks, Aldershot. Eleven months later they landed in France, where they remained throughout the First World War.

Sgt William Brooks, 1st Battalion, on his wedding day shortly before the First World War.
During the war he rose to the rank of sergeant major and was gassed on the western front.
He was a native of Wickham, near Newbury, Berkshire, where his father was a farm bailiff. On
demobilisation he settled down in Chilton Foliat, near Hungerford, becoming a member of the
Parish Council. He also served in the Wiltshire Regiment Territorials. He was a keen gardener and
worked for some years on the Littlecote Estate. Whilst serving he was a member of the regimental
pre-war award-winning championship tug-of-war team.

Richmond Barracks, Dublin, 1907, when the 1st Battalion was inspected by Maj.-Gen. Munro.
These inspections required the whole battalion to demonstrate its effectiveness in many skills. Here
they are being tested on their appearance and turnout in full dress, and their ability to drill at a
very high standard. The battalion passed all tests to the satisfaction of the inspecting officer. The
general was to meet the battalion seven years later when they were part of the 2nd Division under
his command during the retreat from Mons.

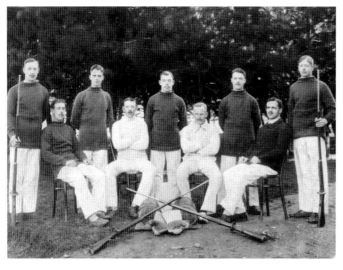

Left: G Company, 1st Battalion bayonet fighting team, winners of the battalion tournament 1910. From left to right, back row: L/Cpl Bullock, L/Cpl Day, Pte Wilkins, Pte Barry, Pte Ballard. Front row: L/Cpl Sawyer, C/Sgt Vesey, Lt Shott DSO, Pte Watts. C/Sgt Vesey was commissioned in 1914 and was killed in action. Lt Shott had an adventurous and varied military career. He fought as a trooper in Col. Plummer's Matabeleland Relief Force in 1896. On the outbreak of the Boer War he went to South Africa and joined Bethune's mounted infantry, serving in operations in Natal, the relief of Ladysmith, and in the actions at Colenso, Spion Kop, Vaal Kranz, Tuela Heights, Laing's Nek and the Orange River Colony. Whilst in South Africa he joined the Royal Berkshire Regiment and at the conclusion of the war was Mentioned in Dispatches three times and awarded the DSO. From 1904 to 1909 he served with the West African Frontier Force which included active service in Northern Nigeria in the Kano-Hadeiga Expedition in 1906, after which he received a further Mention in Dispatches. He served in the 1st Battalion in Ireland and England, getting married in June 1914. Just nine weeks later on 26 August he was killed at the Maroilles Bridge in the battalion's first major action against the Germans during the retreat from Mons. He was the first officer of the regiment to die in the First World War. After the battle he was buried by French civilians in the local cemetery together with seventeen other Royal Berkshire casualties.

Below: The first annual meeting of the Royal Berkshire Old Comrades Association, 25 July 1908, at Brock Barracks, Reading. This gathering of old soldiers included veterans from the Crimea, Afghanistan, Sudan and the Boer War. Although this was the first official gathering, both serving and ex-members of the regiment had actually been meeting since 1903, following a discussion during a break in a route march at Hook Heath

between five sergeants who first suggested the idea. They were Sgts Doubleday, Webb, Lambe, Parsons and C/Sgt London. The first unofficial meeting was held in London and excluded officers, who had their own dinner club. The official organisation was later formed on the initiative of Lt-Col. Gamble, who was unaware of the previous meetings. Sgt Doubleday is seated in uniform on the left. The Regimental Association still meets at Brock Barracks and holds its reunions there every July.

Right: Winners of the Meerut, Assault at Arms competition, 1909, 2nd Battalion, India. From left to right, back row: Pte Buckeridge, Pte Fox. Middle row: L/Cpl Potter, Ptes Dore, Donovan, Dunnett, Bradbury, Cotton. Front row: Sgt Embling, Sgt Maj Quick, L/Cpl Hart. The soldiers on either side wear padded chest protectors and are carrying spring-loaded practice bayonets. Fencing masks were worn during competitions and training sessions. These events were fiercely contested by all companies with the regimental medical officer being fully

employed. Three years later some of the men in this photograph were using bayonets for real on the western front. Sgt-Maj. Quick was captured by the Boers during the Boer War. He went on to become the battalion quartermaster during the First World War. Sgt Embling, who frequently appeared in the medals for bayonet fighting competitions, won a Distinguished Conduct Medal in 1915.

Below: Recruiting was always high on the agenda and the regiment took every opportunity to raise its profile in the county of Berkshire. Here, recruits from the depot re-enact the stand of the last eleven at Maiwand during a carnival in Newbury, around 1911.

Above: Sgt Ernest Doubleday on attachment from the 1st Battalion to a Northern Nigerian Regiment, *c.*1910. He was in charge of an outpost of thirty men at Pirambi. All regiments seconded officers and NCOs to local regiments in different parts of the British Empire. Many volunteered to have postings such as this extended as it gave them a lifestyle unavailable to them within a normal infantry regiment at home. Sergeant Doubleday's servants consisted of one soldier orderly and three boys who came from the Hausas and Fubani tribes. Here he is pictured with the result of a hunting day. He became known to the native soldiers of this regiment as *Serikin Baka* which translates as 'King of Hunters'.

Below: A hunting party of bandsmen from the 2nd Battalion, Sabatu, India, together with their pet dogs and monkeys, *c.*1910. In the back row second from the left is Bandsman George Henry White, whose

time in the Army expired in October 1913, after twelve years of service. He transferred to the Army Reserve and retired to Bath where he took up employment as a gardener. He was recalled on the outbreak of the First World War and was posted to the Somerset Light Infantry. He served throughout the war with the 7th Battalion (SLI), rising to the rank of sergeant. He received a Mention in Dispatches in 1918 and survived the First World War. He returned to civilian life in 1919.

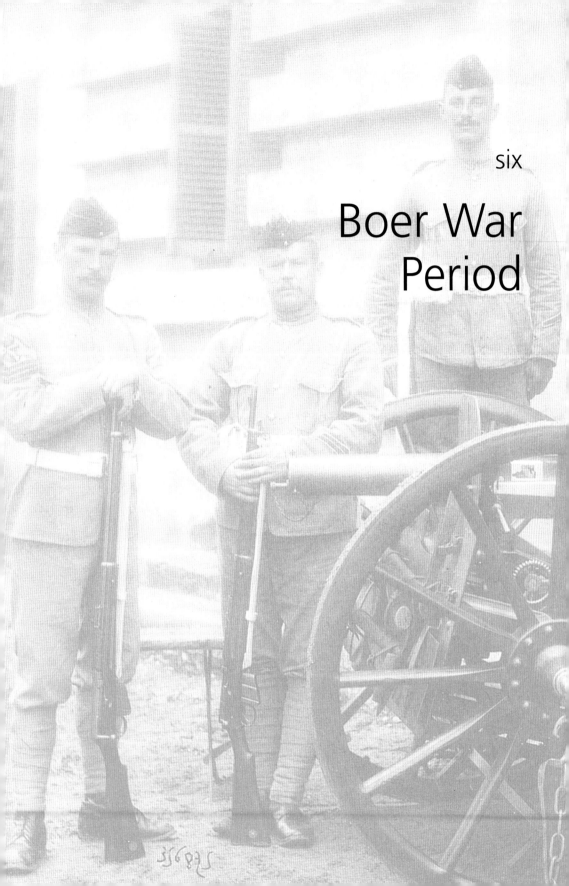

six

Boer War
Period

The officers of the 2nd Battalion, Kings William Town, South Africa, c.1899. The battalion had arrived in South Africa in 1898. This photograph is believed to have been taken just before the departure of the commanding officer, prior to taking up a staff appointment. From left to right, front row: Lt Edward Blunt, Capt. Sir Thomas Pasley, Maj. Frederick McCracken, Lt-Col. Alexander Frazer (CO), Capt. William McClintock, Capt. Reginald Bray, Capt. Richard Macdonnell. Later in the campaign Capt. Pasley, as Pte House's company commander, wrote one of the four recommendation's for the soldier's Victoria Cross.

A very different picture to the one shown above. This features members of C Company, 2nd Battalion, in South Africa, c.1901. As tactics developed during the Boer War, units sometimes, for specific operations, adopted the dress and style of the Boers.

The 2nd Battalion, in shirt sleeves, on a march to Fincham's Nek, *c*.1900. This ground was later described as, 'undulating, thirsty veldt, sand floored, overgrown with brown scrub, along the foot of perpetual kopjes[hills]'. The exact location and date is not known, but from the formation it is clear they are not in immediate danger of being engaged by the Boers. Like all other infantry regiments in the war, the 2nd Battalion took great pride in covering long distances on foot with few men, if any, dropping out.

The 2nd Battalion, in November 1900, with Gen. Gatacre's column (Gen. 'Backacher' to the troops). Here, what is thought to be G and H Companies, under Maj. Bray, take a halt for refreshment during a long, hot and tiring march. Forced marches were a regular feature of the campaign. One such march, of thirty-five miles, undertaken by the 2nd Battalion and finishing at Edenburg, was accomplished in twenty-three hours. The hills in the background are known as kopjes and proved formidable obstacles when guarded by skilled Boer defenders.

A different but welcome form of transport. Soldiers of the 2nd Battalion take part in what was described as a 'Rapid Advance' to Pretoria on 11 July 1900. On arrival they took up a position near the Wonderboom Fort, marching past Lord Roberts on the way. Troops were very vulnerable to Boer attack when travelling by train, as the war progressed the use of the armoured train was developed.

The war artist C.E. Fripp's sketch of the 2nd Battalion escorting a convoy from Pretoria, 25 July 1900. Fripp comments that the escorting troops had just been issued with fresh uniforms. The uniforms did not remain in such pristine condition for long as the convey guide later lost his way during a thunderstorm, causing the column to get bogged down. Two days later the convoy returned to Pretoria. Fripp was well acquainted with the regiment, having painted the action at Tofrek. (See page 42.)

The 2nd Battalion, commanded by Lt-Col. E. Burney, deployed for six weeks in July and August 1901 to guard the railway line from the Orange River to Worcester. They were provided with an armoured train as a mobile column, with which to patrol the line, meeting other mobile columns at various pre-arranged points. The columns consisted of forty detachments that were used not only to guard the train and line when mobile, but also to be dropped of at pre-selected vulnerable points along the line where they would build defensive sangars [rock-like emplacements] to ward off Boer incursions and train wreckers. The photograph shows one such battalion position along the railway line.

Soldiers of the 2nd Battalion ford a river during the operations referred to above. This constant patrolling between the posts along the railway line achieved the aim of disrupting the Boer commandos' movement, and was considered at the conclusion of the operation to have been successful. It was recorded that in spite of the hard work, sickness in the battalion was at an all-time low. This photograph was taken from a passing armoured train.

A group of 2nd Battalion soldiers at Post Drift on the Modder River. A number of mounted infantry units were raised during the course of the war, to which the 2nd Battalion provided two companies plus one smaller detachment. It is thought that the group shown here is from one such company. Cpl Joseph Merson later remembered that being detached from the battalion did not mean a lowering of dress standards and that to do so was at his peril, 'We were camped near Wonderfontein when our outpost was attacked by a band of Boers. We rushed to reinforce the outpost. I didn't have my puttees on and the Sgt asked where they were. I said "Hell, can't we fight without puttees". When the skirmish was over I was called up for insubordination. That's how I was broken in rank, and that's how my medals are marked'.

Sgt H. Reynolds, Distinguished Conduct Medal, 2nd Battalion. He was part of the 13th Mounted Infantry Company under the command of Lt G.P.S. Hunt. They were formed in 1900 and operated in the eastern Transvaal, initially under Gen. Bullock, then later under Gen. Hamilton. On 9 May 1902 a large group of Boers broke through the line at the part where Sgt Reynolds' detachment was posted. He later wrote, 'We were going leisurely along one day when Commandant de Wet and 500 of his men came straight for my section and I got out of his way sharp as I only had 17 all told, and came in on his rear and killed one, captured 2 prisoners with about 10 horses and 8 rifles that were dropped. I did not fire but about 20 rounds, my attention was occupied in watching the enemy movements'. As a result of this action he was Mentioned in Dispatches and awarded the DCM. He went on to tell how no man from his section was killed or wounded, and what a high value he placed on their lives. After the war he moved with the 2nd Battalion to Egypt and then in 1904 returned home to Reading where the photograph was taken. Sadly, whilst on leave he died of disease.

A rifle section, 2nd Battalion, South Africa, in a tented camp shortly after a kit inspection, *c.*1900. Their equipment is laid out and rifles are piled. The piling of rifles in the manner shown was an established routine designed to allow soldiers easy access to their weapons in event of attack.

A rare photograph of a 1-pounder 'Pom-Pom' artillery piece in action. Here the gun is manned by a detachment of the 2nd Battalion, it being the second time that soldiers of the battalion had assumed the role of 'Gunners', the first being at Maiwand twenty years before. One of the Royal Berkshire observers is Maj. Bray. The 37mm, water cooled, 25-round belt-fed gun was one of Sir Hiram Maxim's masterpieces and was originally designed in the 1880s as a machine gun but with a heavier punch and a much longer range. The 1-pound shell had an explosive device to assist in spotting the 'fall of shot'. The gun could be described as a larger version of the Maxim machine gun, which is shown on page 37. The 'Pom-Pom' nickname came from the peculiar sound the gun made when fired.

A signalling station at Nooitgedacht, South Africa, *c.*1901. It was manned by 150 soldiers of C Company 2nd Battalion, under the command of Capt. J. Southey (centre with folded arms). Here they were deployed as 'line of communication' troops in Gen. Smith-Dorrien's force. The troops were contained in a defensive area of approximately 450 square yards. One night in January 1901, the post came under a determined attack from around 300 to 400 Boers. The Berkshires held their ground and by morning the Boers were seen to be drifting away northwards. The attack resulted in L/Cpl Brooks being promoted to sergeant, by direct order of the Commander-in-Chief, in recognition of his excellent conduct during the action. The official history describes this location, '... as admirably entrenched as every other post held by the Royal Berkshire, a Regiment which since the days of McCracken's Hill had been notable for its skill in field fortification'.

B Company, 2nd Battalion, Grahamstown, South Africa, July 1902. Peace was declared on 31 May 1902, but the battalion remained in South Africa until October 1902 when they went to Egypt. In the centre of the second row are Lt B.C. Sparrow and Maj. A.S. Turner.

In January 1901 a draft of 100 men under the command of Lt Bathurst arrived on St Helena from the regimental depot in Reading, to assist in the repatriation of Boer prisoners to South Africa. Unfortunately, events elsewhere dictated that the removal of Prisoners of War was shelved. As a consequence, the detachment remained on St Helena for fourteen months. Lt Bathurst later became the Garrison Adjutant and it was he who instigated his unit's onward movement to South Africa after telegraphing Lord Kitchener. Here we see members of the Royal Berkshire detachment escorting Boer Prisoners of War to Deadwood Camp.

High-profile Boer prisoners under the guard of Sgt Littlewood's Royal Berkshire detachment, St Helena, c.1901. The prisoners signed a copy of this photograph, 'To Sgt C. J. Littlewood, from Commadts Van Heckerk and Elcof Sarel'. Elcof (sitting centre, middle row) was the grandson of Paul Kruger and the son of Commandment Sarl Elcof who led the burgers at Rustenburg. He was captured at Mafeking. He escaped twice whilst in St Helena but, being unable to find a boat, gave himself up on both occasions.

Above: Lt Bathurst's detatchment of the Royal Berkshire Regiment furnishes a Guard of Honour for the visit of Rear-Admiral Moore with Capt. Tempus RN from HMS *Gibraltar*, on St Helena, *c.*1901. The watching dock labourers seem distinctly unimpressed, but were no doubt thankful for a temporary rest from their labours.

Left: The commemorative menu for the send-off dinner for the Volunteers of The Royal Berkshire Regiment on leaving for active service in South Africa with the regiment's 2nd Battalion. The Volunteers served for one year only in South Africa. The dinner was given by the Lord Lieutenant of Berkshire, Lord Wantage, and took place in Reading Town Hall on 1 March 1900. This menu was retained by Sgt William Henry Gillett who came from Abingdon. After serving in South Africa he was discharged on 16 June 1901.

Opposite below: The Volunteer Service Company is inspected by Queen Victoria at her own request, in St George's Hall, Windsor Castle, on 28 February 1900, prior to leaving for South Africa.

Above: The Service Company of the 1st (Volunteer) Battalion Royal Berkshire Regiment at Brock Barracks, prior to embarkation for South Africa to join the regulars of the 2nd Battalion. The Company, consisting of three officers and 113 other ranks, under the command of Capt. A.F. Ewen, arrived just in time to join the 2nd Battalion in the Queen's Birthday Parade at Bloemfontien on 24 May 1900. Their first taste of action came in August when they assumed a position in support of A and B Companies at Zilikat's Nek, where Pte House won his Victoria Cross.

Left: 2nd Lt Athelstan Chamberlayne, 3rd (Militia) Battalion Royal Berkshire Regiment, who served in South Africa with the Volunteer Service Company. He joined the Militia on 23 March 1897 and was on parade when the 3rd Battalion received their new colours in 1898. He is pictured here prior to departure, armed with a revolver and sword. He survived the war and returned to England after a year's service with the 2nd Battalion.

Below: A group of Royal Berkshire Volunteers. This photograph was taken on their return to England on the occasion of the presentation of campaign medal ribbons. The group is believed to have served in South Africa between 1901 and 1902, and was therefore independent of the Service Company. The practice of wearing 'slouch hats' in England was tolerated for a number of years, but ceased just prior to the First World War.

The departure from South Africa of members of the 2nd Battalion Reservists and time-expired men, to England, c.1902. These men are receiving a 'Medical' at the bottom of the gangway prior to boarding the troopship for the journey home. The battalion remained in South Africa until 1902 when it was posted to Egypt.

The Maxim machine-gun section of the 1st Battalion prior to joining the 2nd Battalion in South Africa. The Detachment Commander, Lt Annersley, is at the front of the two machine-gun teams. His platoon sergeant, Sgt London, on the left, was severely wounded at Sanna's Post and returned with a bullet in his shoulder that he carried until the day he died in 1910, aged forty-two. Sgt London was also one of the founding fathers of the Regimental Association.

The Governor of Gibraltar greets the 1st Battalion after their arrival,
2 February 1900. They were quartered in South Barracks, with a detachment
on the north front. The battalion had sailed from Southampton on the
SS *Cephalonia*. Although the battalion had not been mobilised for the Boer
War, many of its officers and soldiers had been drafted to the 2nd as 'battle
casualty' replacements and, in turn, were replaced by newly commissioned
officers and recruits. Duties on Gibraltar were heavy with 130 men being
required each day. One unusual task was the processing through Gibraltar of
over 7,000 Spanish mules to be transported to South Africa. Many of the men
became adept muleteers, adopting colourful language to match.

'The best Signalling section in the British Army' was how the signallers of the
1st Battalion were described in 1901, after achieving a score of 134.33 out of
a possible 135 in the army competition. In 1902 they did even better with
the maximum score. They are seen here with the three principal systems of
signalling in use at the time, the flag, lamp and heliograph. The 5in-heliograph,
shown here on the right of the group, was operated by reflecting sunlight
down a narrow beam. Under good conditions, with sufficiently long lines of
sight, ranges of about seventy miles could be achieved. The officer in charge
(third from left, front row) is Lt E.C. Hunt.

One of the 1st Battalion's two machine-gun sections, Gibraltar, 1901. The officer has a mourning arm band which was worn by all officers for six months after the death of Queen Victoria on 22 January 1901. On 23 and 25 January the battalion played a full part in Gibraltar's mourning ceremonies.

With one section detached to the 2nd Battalion, another needed to be maintained in Gibraltar. Here we see one of the Gibraltar guns practising their gun drills on the 'rock' in 1901. The officer in command is kneeling behind the gun to provide direction, with the remainder of the section providing support in the event of a stoppage. All live firing on Gibraltar at this time was directed out to sea.

The 1st Battalion shooting team, Gibraltar, 1901. This was the very successful team that competed in the Queen's Cup, finishing in the prizes. Second from right, first row: Sgt-Maj. Beesley, who was the top shot with a final score of 100 out of a possible 105. He did particularly well at 600 yards. Sgt-Maj. Beesley was later commissioned and wrote *Reminiscences of an old soldier of the Royal Berkshire Regiment* which was later reproduced in the regimental magazine *China Dragon* and is still used by researchers today. On the outbreak of the First World War in 1914 he helped form the 6th (Service) Battalion.

The 1st Battalion's 'Tofrek' veterans at Gibraltar in 1901. In addition to the fourteen shown here, there were others in the 2nd Battalion in South Africa, the Volunteer Battalion and the regimental depot. The photograph includes Maj. McClintock (seated centre) and Regimental Quartermaster Sergeant Casey (seated second from the right).

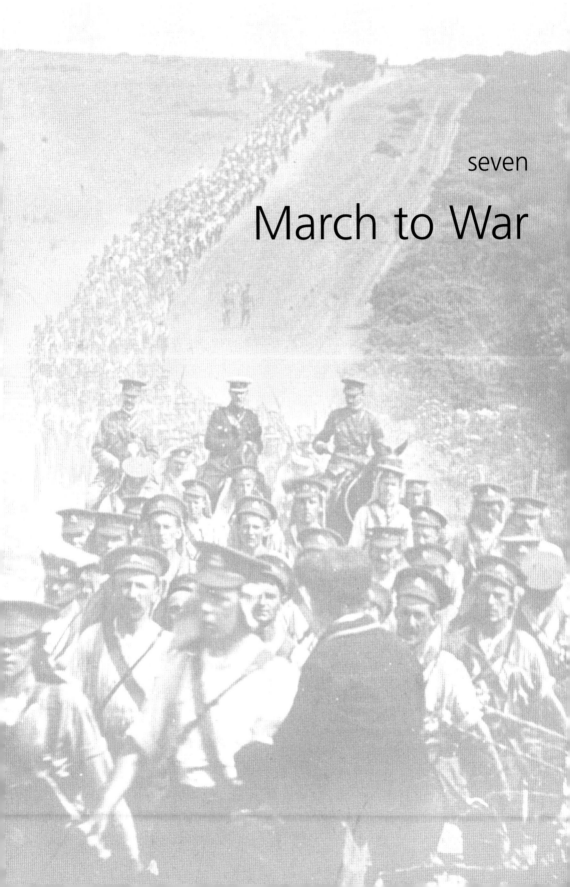

seven

March to War

This photograph shows D Company of the 2nd Battalion at rest whilst on a march near Sabathu (where they were stationed) in India, c.1908. The march routine was governed by resting for ten minutes in every hour. Route marches of sixteen miles in full kit, including 100 rounds of ammunition, were part of the 'Kitchener's' test. The test also included both attack and defence of a position, outpost duties, night operations, field firing, scouting and much more. In 1908 the battalion passed all the tests to the satisfaction of the commander of the 7th Division.

F Company of the 1st Battalion are seen here taking part in the Evelyn-Wood competition in May 1903. The competition required them to march eleven miles in three hours, perform drill on the square, conduct fire discipline and control, and finish up on the range in a shooting competition. Points were awarded for each section. The photograph shows the company dressed in khaki but still with the old 'Slade Wallace' equipment. Unusually for a speed march, they are marching to attention. It could have been to stop them commenting on the fact that they were passing the Jolly Farmer's public house at Runfold near Aldershot without stopping – or for photographic effect!

The 1st Battalion on the march in Southern England in 1903, taking part in Gen. French's manoeuvres. On one occasion the battalion marched from Aldershot to Frensham, Petersfield, Ovington Park, Kingsclere, Newbury and ended up at Hungerford. They marched for twenty hours in 'full marching order' with only three men dropping out. The days were hot and the nights cold with a heavy morning dew. At one stage the battalion halted during a very heavy storm during which several of the hired transport horses died from exhaustion.

The manoeuvres ended up near the Berkshire town of Hungerford, on the downs. Although the exercise had finished there was no question of returning to their barracks at Woking by train; instead they marched to Swallowfield, near Reading, where Gen. French gave them the option of either completing the march to Woking, taking two days with an overnight break at Aldershot, or going the whole way in one day. The commanding officer put it to the men who unanimously chose the latter option. Regimental pride and marching prowess was a major factor in this decision.

Unlike the modern army, there were few weapons for the infantry soldier to master and so the Maxim machine gun presented a unique challenge. Where today each section would be commanded by either a corporal or sergeant, then it was an officer. The photograph shows a Maxim section's cart, upon which would be loaded the ammunition and spare parts and, it is said, the section commander's bottled beer – at least it was in the Royal Berkshires.

The 1st Battalion on the march in 1903 once more, this time a short one from Bordon to Rushmore. Note the 'slouch hats' – these, together with the Slade-Wallace equipment, provide an unusual combination. Also unusually the three officers are carrying rifles, from left to right: Capts Turner, and Cave with Lieut Gosset. During this period the Battalion 'Scouts', under Sgt-Maj. Beesley, were selected to 'trial' three different shades of khaki uniforms so the general staff could select the most appropriate for camouflage. Most of the scouts got to within 200 yards of the generals, with one as close to 100 yards, where he lay undetected for over an hour.

The Delhi Durbar, 1911. The 2nd Battalion played a prominent part in all the proceedings which was reflected in the high percentage of Delhi Durbar medals it gained. The photograph shows the 2nd Battalion marching past (nearest the camera) with the Seaforth Highlanders and King's Royal Rifles were on their left. There were 57,000 troops on parade.

During the Dehli Durbar, members of the 2nd Battalion, in addition to carrying out ceremonial parades, were also responsible for numerous fatigue duties. The Indian Princess who attended the Durbar erected *shamianas*, which were very elaborate tents or temporary shelters. One of the larger and more elegant *shamianas* caught fire and, despite heroic attempts to save it by members of the battalion, was burnt to the ground. Here we see soldiers from the 2nd Battalion picking through the remains of the tent, after which they erected another one in record time. Many fragments of the *shamiana* made their way back to Berkshire in the kitbags of time-expired soldiers as souvenirs.

A mounted infantry course on parade at Amballa, India, 1907. The 2nd Battalion sent two sections of twenty men each on the four-month-long course. The first few weeks were devoted to basic riding skills. The second part of the course included the mastering of the 'closed manege' where, without stirrups and with folded arms, two jumps and a sharp turn had to be negotiated. It goes without saying that contact with the hard Indian earth was frequent. The regiment acquitted itself well, however, winning most of the competitions.

A maxim gun crew and rifle section of the 1st Battalion, Ireland, 1907. From left to right: Ptes Hiscock and Smith, CSIM Reed, Ptes White, Heyburn, Stone, Sumner, Hayes and Simmonds, Cpl Smith. Behind the gun: Ptes Berry and Bailey and Lt Benjamin Gonville Bromhead. Another member of his family won the Victoria Cross at Rorke's Drift with the 24th Foot in 1879. He was with the regiment for many years. In the South African War he served as a Special Service Officer with the Rhodesian Field Force and with Thorneycroft's Mounted Infantry. He went to France in 1914 but was badly wounded shortly after arriving. He died in 1939. His son followed him into the regiment and in 1956 became the last commanding officer of the 1st Battalion prior to its amalgamation with the 1st Battalion Wiltshire Regiment three years later.

Right: The 1st Battalion during the Dublin Manoeuvres, 1907. They are led by the Corps of Drums who carry their instruments on their backs as the battalion marches 'at ease'. The commanding officer, Lt-Col. McClintock, is on foot just behind the drums.

Below: The 1st Battalion officers' mess in the field during the Irish Command Manoeuvres, 12 September 1907. Centre: facing the camera is Commanding Officer Lt-Col. McClintock. Also present at the table (wearing a peaked cap and white arm band) is a Russian military observer. Secrecy about the unit's identity was not an issue at this time, as is shown by the battalion's name emblazoned across the officers' mess wagon.

The machine-gun section of the 1st Battalion rest next to the gun limber. All members of this team are wearing the short-lived 'slouch hat' and visible on their uniform shoulders is the regimental title 'Royal Berkshire', with the number '1' just below. At this time the battalion was stationed in Dublin.

Machine gunners of the 1st Battalion mount their Maxim on a wall during the 1907 manoeuvres in Ireland. The Colour Sergeant holding the gun would have acted as a fire controller. At this time each battalion was equipped with two machine guns.

An informal group of 1st Battalion soldiers at Kilbride Camp, Ireland, *c.*1907. They have piled arms in the traditional way, ready for immediate use. From here they marched through the mountains to a country house called Powerscourt, where they camped in the grounds for a week.

Soldiers of the 2nd Battalion 'digging in' at Jhansi, India, early 1914. Although they practised open warfare tactics, the lessons learned during the Boer War were still fresh in the minds of the more senior officers and other ranks. Little did these men know that they would be digging in earnest within a few months. The photograph was probably taken during a 'Kitchener's test exercise'.

The 1st Battalion machine gunners, Aldershot, 1913, after winning the Eastern Command machine gun challenge cup and shield. The battalion team beat the Rifle Brigade by one point. From left to right, back row: Pte Prior, L/Cpl Greenough, Ptes Arnold and Quelch, L/Cpls Gibbs and Fisher. Middle row: Ptes Greenough, Crockford and Young, Lt Frizell, Lt-Col. Graham, Sgt Smith, Cpl Cooper, L/Cpl Harris, (another) L/Cpl Harris. Front row: Pte Willers, L/Cpl Cortland. Sgt Smith won the Distinguished Conduct Medal in 1914 and was commissioned in 1918. The gun shown is the recently introduced Vickers .303in water-cooled Mk1. It was to remain as the infantry's standard medium machine gun until the early 1960s.

2nd Battalion Machine Gun section, Jhansi, June 1913. From left to right, back row: Ptes Hignell, Boshier, Odey, Fawcett, Pocock and Dean. Front row: Ptes Cooling, Saunders, Baigent, Sgt Hancock, Lt Nugent, L/Cpl Vaughan, Ptes Haynes, Bailey and Wheeler. All infantry battalions prior to the First World War were equipped with two machine guns. After the outbreak of the First World War, when the full enormity of the threat became apparent, the machine-gun capability was substantially increased, leading to the formation of the Machine Gun Corps, with many of the battalion's machine gunners transferring into that corps.

Young buglers of the 4th Battalion practise their skills under Drum Major Davey at the battalion's annual camp in 1910. The battalion's Corps of Drums achieved a high standard of proficiency under Drum Major Davey, but because of his age and despite his protest, he was not allowed to accompany them to France during the First World War. Instead he was transferred to the newly formed 2nd/4th Battalion to work his familiar magic there, before they, too, were sent to France.

Two soldiers of the 1st (Volunteer) Battalion at annual camp near the Bustard Inn on Salisbury Plain, 1904. All volunteer units were required to attend an annual camp to complete their extended training programme. The 1st (Volunteer) title disappeared in 1908, as part of the Haldane Army reforms, to become the 4th (Territorial Force) Battalion Royal Berkshire Regiment. The change was designed to help establish closer ties with the regular battalions. Here we see the soldiers with two transport mules which have been supplied under contract by Mr G. Hanbury. Most of the animals were supplied under contract, it being unrealistic to have them on permanent 'charge'.

Rivers, even the smallest ones, present infantry soldiers with formidable obstacles. As a consequence, crossing them is a skill that requires constant practice. Whilst stationed in Ireland in 1907, the 1st Battalion were tasked to cross the 138ft-wide river Liffey. Here we see A and B Companies constructing a trestle and barrel-pier bridge. It took 9½ hours uninterrupted labouring to complete the task. Other members of A Company are preparing to 'raft' some equipment across the river. At that time A Company was under the command of Maj. Harcourt-Taylor, who died shortly afterwards. He had been present in all the regiment's actions in the Sudan and South Africa.

The Machine Gun section of the 1st Battalion ferry one of their two Maxim guns across the river Liffey on their self-constructed raft, 1907.

Drum Major Davey and his buglers lead the 4th Battalion march out of camp for field training at Lulworth in 1913. The drums would play the battalion out of, and back to, camp. The hot conditions are apparent by the wearing of neck protectors. Drum Major Davey served in the regiment as a volunteer from 1883 to 1917, when age caught up with him.

The marching column of the 4th Battalion at the annual camp, Lulworth, 1913. This was the last but one camp before the start of the First World War. All the troops are in shirt sleeve order, wearing neck protection against the fierce sun. In keeping with the traditions of the army as a whole at this time, it was a point of honour to keep the 'dropping out rate' as low as possible.

A group of 1st Battalion soldiers march into Lydd, Kent, in the summer of 1911. They had marched the thirty miles from Dover in two days, with an overnight halt at Shorncliffe. On arrival they moved on to the ranges to complete their annual range classification course, an important event for them as it affected their pay. Fifteen well-aimed shots a minute was the norm. Three years later their shooting and marching skills were severely put to the test in the 'Retreat from Mons'.

In India, in early 1914, the 2nd Battalion was also on the march. Here a group are seen after preparing a meal during a halt. Unlike England, where meal breaks could sometimes be arranged at a convenient barracks en route, in India everything had to be taken with them. Marches were usually started very early to avoid the heat of the day. Some of the pots and utensils seen in the photograph will be familiar to those serving today, as the same types are still being issued. By the end of 1914 the battalion was in France on the Western Front, where it was to remain until the end of the war.

THE ROYAL BERKS PLAYING THE ROYAL GUARD TO KING GEORGE V 1914.

On 16 April 1914 the 1st Battalion took part in its last but one public parade prior to the outbreak of the First World War, furnishing a Guard of Honour for King George V at the Royal Pavilion during his majesty's visit to Aldershot. The band and Corps of Drums are seen here heading the Guard of Honour back to Mandora Barracks after the parade.

B Company of the 1st Battalion march past the saluting dais, in line, on the occasion of the King's Birthday Review at Aldershot in 1914. Little did the officers and soldiers of this company realise that within a few weeks they would be engaged in a very different march – the Retreat from Mons. On 25 August 1914 B Company, under the command of Maj. A.S. Turner, engaged the advancing Germans in the battalion's first major action of the war on the bridge at Maroilles. At the conclusion of this action, Maj. Turner was captured and sixty-one other ranks were killed, wounded or missing.

Other titles published by Tempus

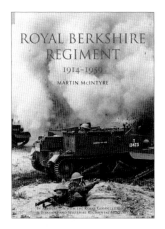

Royal Berkshire Regiment 1914–1959
MARTIN MCINTYRE

The Museum of the Royal Gloucestershire, Berkshire and Wiltshire Regiment contains many thousands of photographs. In this detailed and informative book, Martin McIntyre relates the history of the Royal Berkshire Regiment from 1914–59. Martin McIntyre is a volunteer at the Regimental Museum in Salisbury and a former member of the Duke of Edinburgh's Royal Regiment.
0 7524 3085 8

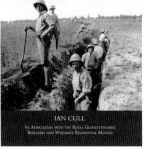

The 2nd Battalion Royal Berkshire Regiment in World War One
IAN CULL

The 2nd Royal Berkshire Regiment were a fighting force of hardened professionals recalled from guarding the Empire to face the German onslaught in August 1914. Encountering weather conditions they were unaccustomed to, trench warfare and tropical diseases, they found themselves in a war unlike anything they had ever trained for. Following Neuve Chapelle, the Somme and a surprise German attack near the Aisne in 1918, they were almost obliterated by the end of the war. This book covers the few short years between 1911 and 1919.
0 7524 3085 8

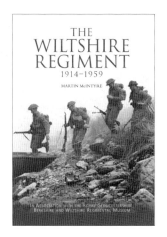

The Wiltshire Regiment 1914–1959
MARTIN MCINTYRE

Focusing on the period between the First World War and 1959, the date of the regiment's amalgamation with the Royal Berkshire Regiment when they formed the Duke of Edinburgh's Royal Regiment (Berkshire and Wiltshire), this painstakingly researched book uses over 200 photographs to vividly document the Wiltshire Regiment's role in many campaigns and battles from the trenches on the Western Front to terrorists in Cyprus in 1959, from Shanghai through to the Second World War.
0 7524 3085 8

If you are interested in purchasing other books published by Tempus, or in case you have difficulty finding any Tempus books in your local bookshop, you can also place orders directly through our website

www.tempus-publishing.com